Also by Michael Maron

Michael Maron's Instant Makeover Magic

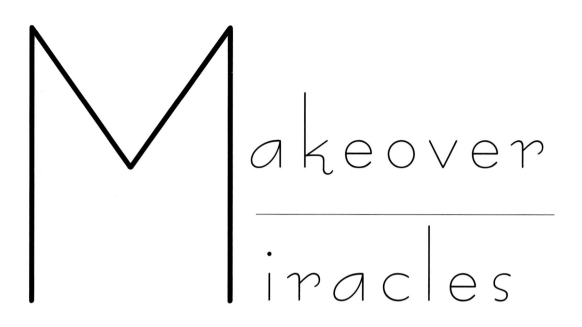

Makeover Miracles

A Before-and-After Guide to Corrective Makeup, Cosmetic Surgery, and Anti-Aging Strategies

Michael Maron

Photography by Michael Maron

Crown Publishers, Inc.
New York

To Judy Gray,
who has taught me
the true definition
of beauty: love,
compassion, humor,
and self-worth.

A portion of the royalties of this book will be donated by the author to The Phoenix Society for Burn Survivors, Inc., and Operation Smile International.

Published by Crown Publishers, Inc., 201 East 50th Street, New York, New York 10022. Member of the Crown Publishing Group.

Random House, Inc. New York, Toronto, London, Sydney, Auckland

CROWN is a trademark of Crown Publishers, Inc.

Manufactured in Hong Kong

Design by Lauren Dong

Library of Congress Cataloging-in-Publication Data
Maron, Michael
     Makeover miracles/Michael Maron.
        p.   cm.
     Index.
     1. Beauty, Personal. 2. Cosmetics. 3. Surgery, Plastic.
4. Face—Surgery.   I. Title.
RA776.98.M37 1994
646.7'042—dc20   93-12100
                                CIP

ISBN 0-517-58430-1

10 9 8 7 6 5 4 3 2 1

First Edition

Contents

Preface

She was the most beautiful girl I had ever seen. I barely ever took my eyes off of her. The problem was she never knew I existed. After all, we were only nine, she was shy, and I was a nerd. For hours, I'd draw pictures of Sandie Davis as she sat across the room in my fourth-grade class. I even drew from memory, with her likeness embedded in my thoughts. I was mesmerized by her eyes . . . the tilt of her small nose . . . the shape of her lips. I felt nobody could see her beauty as I did. Maybe nobody else did. Little did I know my fascination for beauty was starting then.

I lived right around the corner from Knott's Berry Farm, which then was literally a berry farm with a few rides and free admission and now is a mega-amusement park in Southern California. My favorite thing about the park was the portrait artists who drew faces in pastel. As a youngster, I would stand there for hours looking over their shoulders as they'd re-create the image of the face sitting before them. It was magic. I witnessed true masters of chiaroscuro—an artist's technique of arranging light and shadow to create form. I was fascinated to see that as they delicately blended one pastel over another, each color instantly became an entirely new shade. The sketches became so real and lifelike, they seemed to move. I learned what it is about a face that gives it its own individuality. I learned more about faces at Knott's than in any art class. And

before long, I could sketch the same way.

I became a professional portrait artist by the age of twelve. I always loved faces and actually thought everyone "saw" the face as I did. Later on, photography became a natural extension for me. I was able to use lighting to control the light and shadow on the hills and valleys of a face. I could create a perfect landscape . . . with the face being eternally captured for one moment in time.

But it wasn't until I learned how equally effective makeup could be to redefine and improve the face that my real fascination began. I studied makeup day after day, practicing and experimenting on models. I began to shape the images of "potential" models, transforming them into cover girls, and giving them each their *own* "look."

I continued my career as a fashion and beauty photographer for years to follow. Wearing two hats, I always did the makeup for every client I photographed.

Because of my love for possibility and promise, the process of transformation continued to fascinate me. Although my clientele grew to include some of the most beautiful and famous faces in the world, my real passion was my desire to help those who weren't necessarily used to looking beautiful—maybe someone who never wore makeup before in her life, or a woman in her seventies, or someone with less-than-perfect skin or irregular features, or a person who was tragically burned over 80 percent of her body. I learned to recognize a person's beauty potential.

I became more concerned about making my client look good and less concerned about what color was "in" or what was "out." For me, the real challenge in makeup is knowing how to use corrective measures to improve specific problems and how to obtain maximum improvement with the least amount of obvious attention to the makeup itself. I began to specialize in the art of corrective makeup—and in a sense, became a "corrective makeup therapist"—something that has become an inspirational experience for me.

So, why am I writing a book that includes the subject of cosmetic surgery? Because cosmetic surgery has become everyone's right. More than an estimated 1 million Americans undergo cosmetic surgery every year. No longer are face-lifts the province of movie stars. In fact, a recent survey shows that approximately 30 percent of those who elect to have cosmetic surgery have family incomes of less than $25,000 a year. Cosmetic surgery has become as common as a visit to the beauty salon and far more convenient than in the past.

It's rare that the subject of cosmetic surgery doesn't come up when I'm working on someone's face, and it seems everyone has something about his or her appearance that he or she would like to hide or improve upon. There probably isn't an individual who hasn't thought about how he or she might look if this or that were fixed. Even Princess Diana has been quoted as saying, "I'd like to get my conk [nose] fixed."

Though cosmetic surgery is a constant topic for the media, the overabundance of conflicting information can leave the public as confused as before. Oftentimes, reports on the subject are sensationalized with a focus on "horror stories" associated with bad surgery. Don't get me wrong, it's important and necessary to have as much information as possible. In fact, with growing public awareness and caution, fewer unfortunate results are likely to occur. A recent survey, however, has shown that 90 percent of patients who have undergone elective cosmetic surgery said they were satisfied and 82 percent said they'd do it again. Most books on the subject, as excellently written as some may be, are too clinical, contain too much text, and lack high-quality, attractive photography. I feel there's a need for a book that the general public can identify with.

As a makeup consultant to the American Society of Plastic and Reconstructive Surgeons, my experience with doctors has been invaluable. I attend many of their annual meetings, and I speak at various medical functions and symposiums. In fact, it was at my first speaking engagement for cosmetic surgeons that I realized how much our very different crafts complement each other, and how the union of the two is giving way to a new era. Now I'm even invited to "scrub-in" on surgeries.

Currently, I consult privately with clients on cosmetic surgery as much as I do makeup. I love examining the varying techniques of masterful surgeons. If I had known years ago what I know now, I may have chosen to become a cosmetic surgeon. I marvel at their abilities and have great respect for their artistry. I've seen them perform miracles.

I'm very grateful for my affiliation with the medical community and my hands-on experience with patients. This dovetailing of efforts has given me the opportunity to share realistic and impartial, up-to-date information. In addition, it's enabled me to *show* results in an easy-to-understand and nontechnical fashion. My purpose in discussing cosmetic surgery is to demystify the subject and help alleviate many of the fears associated with it. Most important, I now can help bridge the gap between the art of cosmetic surgery and the art of corrective makeup. Maybe I can even help make someone's dream come true.

I never dreamed that drawing faces in elementary school would lead to such a rewarding career. And, Sandie Davis became Homecoming Queen.

Introduction: More than Just a Pretty Face

A blemish in the soul cannot be corrected in the face;
but a blemish in the face,
if corrected, can refresh the soul.
—JEAN COCTEAU

The Marriage of Corrective Makeup and Cosmetic Surgery

Southern California, THE beauty mecca of the United States, led the way in the beauty revolution during the 1980s. My previous book, *Michael Maron's Instant Makeover Magic*, revealed Hollywood celebrities without their makeup. It was one of the first of its kind because it made every woman feel better about herself by showing that no one is perfect. Now, a decade later, I'm going to take you on a more intensive beauty journey.

This book visually demonstrates the cosmetic industry's latest techniques of corrective makeup and the breakthroughs in facial cosmetic surgery, one of modern medicine's most sophisticated crafts. The marriage of the two can create optimum results for today's look and is only the beginning of the miracles that await us in the future.

SELF-IMAGE

The desire to be attractive is a basic human instinct. We all primp before dates or meetings with strangers, take last minute glances while passing by windows, and check ourselves out in the reflection of a friend's sunglasses.

But today, wanting to look good goes beyond the need to attract a mate. It's become a necessity as we all struggle up the job ladder. Research has shown that attractive people are seen as more sociable, poised, and outgoing. They're known to win more prestigious and higher-paying jobs, achieve preferential treatment from their doctors and teachers, and even attain shorter jail sentences! Psychologists have concluded that those who look and feel their best are happier and live longer than those who don't. Bottom line: Good looks elicit a positive response, and beauty can very much be its own reward.

A recent study of female subjects showed that more than 90 percent were dissatisfied with their looks. Many people are so self-conscious about an aspect of their looks that it inhibits their lives in some way.

Beauty is indeed in the eye of the beholder, but it's also in the eye of the possessor. What actually makes us attractive to others is our projection of our self-esteem.

'BEAUTY PSYCHOTHERAPY'

It stands to reason that most people who feel good about themselves take better care of themselves and consequently look better. But I've found this theory works in reverse as well. My beauty makeover sessions in women's prisons have proven to me that as the inmates began to look better, they tended to feel better about themselves.

By working from the outside in, the inmates' appearances improved, as did their emotional well-being, which also effected a positive attitude from others. You might say that the repair of the physical is a rejuvenation of the spirit. I call this "beauty psychotherapy."

IT'S OKAY TO BE BEAUTIFUL

If you have this book in your hands, no doubt you're seeking ways to look your very best. If you deny your desire to be attractive, you're probably unaware of your inherent potential. Oftentimes, we make excuses about why we can't do something positive for ourselves. We say things like,

"it's vain," or "it's tampering with God's given handiwork."

First, know that it's okay to be beautiful. You may feel you're too fat, too thin, too old, too busy, too whatever. What you're really saying is you don't deserve to be beautiful. But you do deserve to be the best you possibly can. Beauty has to be a place where you come from, not go to. And total beauty must be a combination of the mental, emotional, spiritual, and the physical, for looks alone can never compete with attitude, brains, talent, and the love in one's heart.

THE MIRACLE OF CHANGE

This book will show you what cosmetic options are available today. Because of the continuing advancements in modern cosmetic treatments, endless possibilities and solutions are available to improve your physical shortcomings and bring new order to your appearance.

I'm not advocating change for the sake of change. I'm advocating choice. If you have something that bothers you, why not do something about it and liberate yourself from the problem? Today, you don't have to settle for blotchy skin, sun-induced wrinkles, a misshapen nose, or droopy eyelids.

Be careful though, not to forget who you are. Paying too much attention to your "physical package" and ignoring the real you can do harm.

Psychotherapist Dr. Wayne Dyer says it best in his book *You'll See It When You Believe It.* "The container cannot give you the pleasure and satisfaction and nourishment that the contents do. Even though you cannot see what is inside that beautiful package, you know that whatever it is provides you with important irreplaceable nourishment. A lifetime of focusing exclusively on the package will result in a spiritually undernourished and quite unhappy you."

Though physical beauty may be skin deep, the feeling of being unattractive goes beyond. I've learned that there are no minor blemishes—particularly when they're on *your* face. And my heart goes out to the facially disfigured who suffer unfair discrimination. When I asked my client Jennifer, whose face has severe burn scars, how she feels when she hears her girlfriends complain about a few blemishes, she responded, "I understand . . . that's *their* scar" (see bottom left photograph, page 60).

YOUR OWN BEAUTY POTENTIAL

This book is divided into three parts that should be followed in sequence. You must first gain a basic understanding about the proportions of your face (Part I) before you learn about the many possibilities and solutions of corrective makeup (Part II). Then you'll explore facial cosmetic surgery and see how various surgical procedures can be complemented with makeup to achieve some amazing results (Part III).

The pages ahead are filled with more than 200 photographs. Maybe you'll see a little bit of yourself in one of them. I personally photographed most of the subjects, documenting their metamorphosis from "before" to "after." This way, the effects of change could be seen under the exact lighting and in the same position. (In a few cases, photographs were provided by doctors.) Retouching of photographs was never used to alter a makeover.

I also made a special attempt to avoid a posed or "glamour" look on the "after" photos. And, although hair is an important element in beautification, I asked most of the subjects to have their hair off their faces, so that you can see that the results are due to makeup or surgery alone or the combination of both. I never want to mislead you into thinking the effect of the makeover is attributed to the hairstyle.

It was important to me to photograph the "before" photos exactly the way subjects arrived at my studio. I found that some women never had worn makeup prior to their transformation. Their reasons ranged from lack of makeup know-how to feeling their skin was too wrinkled or their eyes too "baggy," to just not having had any prior incentive.

I'm convinced this book will allow you to view your face differently than you've ever done before. You'll learn how to analyze your facial structure and how to use corrective makeup to enhance your strengths as well as play down your weaknesses. You'll see how your face ages, how to look years younger, and even how to combat the aging process. You'll even learn if corrective makeup can be an alternative to cosmetic surgery.

Facial cosmetic surgery procedures are explained in a simple and understandable way. You'll see actual examples of temporary marks or discolorations you might expect immediately after a procedure—marks that doctors rarely show to their patients. You'll learn about some fascinating corrective cosmetics you may never have heard of before and how to use makeup for immediate post-surgery cover-up, so that you can resume your normal activities quickly. I also demonstrate how to adjust your makeup to your "new" face. If you're considering surgery, this book will help you increase your awareness about surgical procedures so that you can become a better informed patient, and communicate more effectively with your doctor.

The no-nonsense information you'll obtain here will give you an arsenal of easy corrective makeup techniques for future "emergencies." And, you'll get answers to specific appearance-related problems that usually go unaddressed. Finally, you'll be able to see your own beauty potential to enable you to be all you can be.

Cosmetic surgery should be taken very seriously. This book doesn't discuss *every* possibility and risk involved with any given procedure. And, although I may be knowledgeable about facial cosmetic surgery, I don't perform surgery and am not a doctor. (Any medical or health matter should always be consulted with a physician.) My aim is to share with you the information I've gleaned from scores of the world's leading doctors and to assist you in achieving the looks you've always wanted.

I hope this book will help you feel comfortable about improving your appearance. It can make that life-changing difference you deserve. I wish you luck and support you on your quest for beauty. Remember, makeover miracles happen all the time and they can happen to you

Michael Maron

Part I

Beauty—"Measuring Up"

Beauty is a far
greater recommendation than any
letter of introduction.
— ARISTOTLE

Chapter 1

The face of Today

Beauty—it's only a concept

Webster defines beauty as "the quality or aggregate of qualities in a person or thing that gives pleasure to the senses or pleasurably exalts the mind or spirit." Beauty is intangible, based on a personal response rather than a set ideal. But did you know that we unconsciously determine whether a new acquaintance is attractive or not in less than ten seconds?

Studies have been conducted with infants, who when shown pairs of photographs of attractive and unattractive faces, tended to stare longer at the more attractive face. Race, age, or sex of the people in the photographs didn't seem to affect their choice. These studies suggest that the perception of beauty may be inborn.

An in-depth study among college students showed that in our society, regardless of sex or race, most attractive faces have similar characteristics. Women that were determined to be attractive to the opposite sex had more childlike features that included large eyes, small, rounded noses and chins, full lips, and smooth skin. The younger, more childlike features produced a positive, caretaking response as well as a perception of better health and youth. Prominent cheekbones and narrow cheeks, which are mature features, were also considered attractive.

The combination of two opposing types of features—such as baby-faced and mature—were deemed by women to be attractive qualities of the male face. The most consistently desirable features on men were large eyes, prominent cheekbones, a medium to smaller-sized nose, a strong chin, and thick eyebrows. As with females, a wide smile was rated more attractive, but, on men, a great smile tended to overcome something like a huge nose. In both men and women, the width of the nose at the nostrils was related to attractiveness, while the

Faces like these
scored high in attractiveness:
large eyes, small nose, high cheekbones,
and smooth skin.

ences we all possess. But in order to bring out that *je ne sais quoi*—that indescribable something—it's necessary to learn how to maximize or minimize what we have.

nose size was found to be of less consequence on men. Neither the height of the forehead, the darkness of hair, nor skin color was related to attractiveness.

TWENTY-FIRST-CENTURY BEAUTY

We're constantly being bombarded by new trends, to the extent that if we were to follow them all, we'd never have a chance to retain our individuality. I love change, but not for the sole purpose of going along with fashion.

As we approach the twenty-first century, our standards of feminine beauty are changing. The imagined "ideal" has disappeared. There's no certain "correct" look, and women, thank goodness, are finally able to express their individuality. The face of today is a natural one, with ethnic characteristics being maintained. More and more, terms such as "unusual," "exotic," "striking," or even "handsome" are used to describe beautiful women. Attractiveness doesn't only mean young, blond, light-eyed, or small-nosed. We've learned to appreciate the wonderful differ-

facial harmony

Have you ever heard the saying "the eye sees many things of which the mind takes no notice"? Have you ever looked at someone's face, or your own for that matter, and known something is askew, without knowing what it is specifically? You may have always thought your nose is too long, when in fact, because of a short or receding chin, the length of your nose is emphasized. This is due to a lack of *symmetry*. Symmetry is beauty resulting from balanced proportions. If you ever wondered how you might look with somebody else's features, with Elizabeth Taylor's nose, for example, think again. Facial features can only be attractive if they're in harmony with the rest of your face. In fact, the word *cosmetics* is derived from the Greek word *kosmetikos,* which means skilled in adornment and having order and harmony. No face is perfectly symmetrical. But, facial features can be improved upon if desired.

the three elements of facial attractiveness

If the nose of Cleopatra had been a little shorter, the whole face of the world would have been changed.

—BLAISE PASCAL

When you think of the legendary beauties, those with style and élan such as Greta Garbo or Sophia Loren, or contemporary beauties such as Cher and Julia Roberts, they all have faces with one-of-a-kind features. Their nonconforming looks make them unforgettable, as well as beautiful.

Facial features are one of three elements that constitute physical beauty. **Skin texture** is another. But physical beauty actually goes clear to the bone, for the **bone structure** is the third element. Each person has an individual "facial architecture." It's important for me to say again that there's no such thing as a perfect face, nor should one strive to have one. In fact, distinctive features give a face more character and are far more interesting. They're not boring.

The beauty of your face is the sum of its parts. Only by analyzing the symmetry of your face can you learn to maximize your assets and play down your imperfections.

The 1930s film star Marlene Dietrich was an expert at self-analysis. When she came to Hollywood, her face was round and full. She is said to have had her molars removed to emphasize her cheekbones. She created her trademark arched eyebrows by dramatically tweezing her low, nondistinctive ones. She studied every facet of her face and used endless professional cosmetic tricks to transform herself into one of Hollywood's most fabled beauties. Norma Jean Baker did the same. At twenty-three, with a little help from a cosmetic surgeon, she had the tip of

her nose refined and her chin made slightly bigger. With the added illusion of makeup, she redefined her look and became Marilyn Monroe.

Like those great stars, you must first learn to understand your face before you can make the most of what you have. Then you can decide how you want to attain your most flattering look.

face analysis

The Egyptians were the first to describe mathematical measurements of the face for the purpose of establishing facial aesthetics. The ancient Greeks used this same criteria, as did Leonardo da Vinci and, in this century, famed makeup expert Max Factor. Indeed, Factor used an instrument called a "facial calibrator" to measure the faces of the leading ladies he enhanced.

Before you can assess your face, you must first have some guidelines of aesthetic balance from which to draw. I prefer using the term "well-balanced face" instead of "ideal" or "perfect" face, because the latter two words connote something better-than. I call the facial assessment process *face analysis.*

Don't worry about determining your face shape. Most people are a combination of shapes anyway. Trying to create a "perfect oval" is nonsense, since an oval face doesn't have the significance of being ideal that it may have had in the past. In fact, because it has less skeletal support, the oval face actually ages faster than a square-jawed or round face! (See "Having a Youthful Edge," page 75.)

You're about to take one of the most important steps to help you improve your appearance. Don't fret if your measurements fall outside the well-balanced face. Rarely does anyone "measure up." The purpose of face analysis is to allow you to understand your own facial proportions so that you can see your face in a more objective and scientific way. This will help you determine

HORIZONTAL FACIAL PROPORTIONS

the reason why a particular feature may appear disconcerting. Remember, though, that sometimes playing up the very thing that is unique about your face can be an asset.

Before you start your own face analysis, I want you to pull your hair back and completely remove all your makeup. Leave your ego aside, and take an objective, scrutinizing look in the mirror (you'll need two mirrors to check your profile). Use a small ruler to measure.

Note: Photographs of yourself can also be very helpful: Take one looking straight ahead and another in profile (be sure to have your hairline showing).

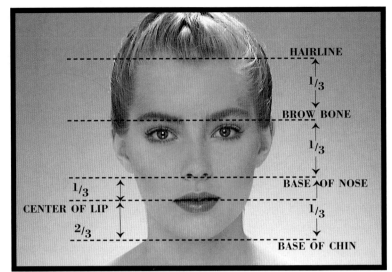

The well-balanced face can be divided equally into horizontal thirds. The bottom third can also be divided into thirds. Your nose could appear long if middle third is greater than upper or lower thirds. Your chin could appear large if lower third is greater.

*M*athematics in beauty—measurements of the well-balanced face

EYE PLACEMENT

The well-balanced face equally divides into vertical fifths, which should be five times the length of one eye. The distance between the eyes should be equal to the width of one eye. If the eyes are close-set, they're less than one eye length apart. If they're wide-set eyes, they're greater than one eye length apart.

NOSE PLACEMENT

The outside of the nostrils should approximately line up with the inner corners of the eyes. The sides of the nose should form a continuous line which slopes into the brow line. Any breakup of this line can distort the mid-face (the middle third of the face) contour. (The total area of the nose should be less than 5 percent of the facial area.)

MOUTH PLACEMENT

The width of the mouth should be equal to the inner edge of the irises (the distance between the colored portion) of the eyes. A long mouth is greater than this distance. A short mouth is less than this distance. The two peaks that form the cupid's bow of the upper lip should start at a point directly down from the center of each nostril. Generally, the upper lip is thinner than the

VERTICAL FACIAL PROPORTIONS

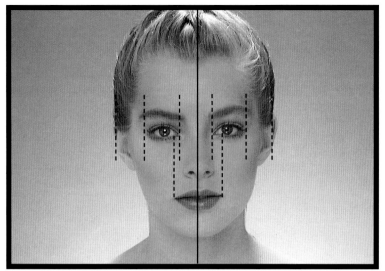

The well-balanced face can be divided equally into vertical fifths equal to the length of one eye. To analyze facial symmetry, draw an imaginary line down center of face. This establishes an axis line where midline points should lie. See if line passes through center of tip of nose, through middle of crest (cupid's bow) of upper lip, to center of chin. Midline symmetry is rarely perfect.

lower lip. The width of the mouth should be approximately equal to the distance from the center of the lips to the base of the chin and should be half the width of the face at mouth level.

THE WELL-BALANCED PROFILE

In profile, facial features form angles that help determine balance and symmetry. The forehead, nose, lips, and chin are interdependent. **The Aesthetic Triangle** is formed by connecting the features with straight lines. (See photographs, page 20.) Most women have smaller features than men and the profile usually appears less bold. Women's lips generally appear more prominent and fuller than men's. The upper lip should protrude over the lower lip a bit, and have a slight pout. Men's upper lips are generally flatter than women's. The chin should project almost as

far as the lower lip. Men's chins are usually slightly stronger. Receding chins are generally considered more feminine and childlike.

Men's noses are typically larger and have a higher bridge than women's; both characteristics are considered to be more masculine. A woman's face, however, tolerates a more masculine nose better than a man's face tolerates a feminine nose.

A well-balanced nose should meet the forehead at a point between the upper eyelashes and the eye's crease (the fold of the eyelid), forming a slight break or indentation. This indentation is usually greater in men, creating more projecting brows.

The nose should have a subtle depression just prior to the tip so that it turns up slightly. This is generally less pronounced for men.

Women's noses should form a 35-degree angle at the bridge, and for men, an angle up to approximately 40 degrees. The tip angle for women should be approximately 45 degrees. Men's tip angles are normally less.

The nasal angle (where the bottom of the nose meets the upper lip) should be approximately 90 degrees or more for women. Greater than 90 degrees for men could appear too upturned or childlike. (The angle of the nostrils should be between 95 and 105 degrees for women and between 90 and 95 degrees for men.)

The length of the base (underside) of the nose should be approximately the same as the length of the distance from the upper lip. (Fifty to 60 percent of the tip should fall in front of a vertical line adjacent to the most projecting portion of the lips.)

THE AESTHETIC TRIANGLE

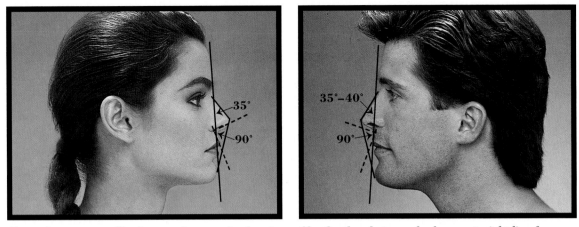

To analyze your profile, have a photograph taken in profile. On the photograph, draw a straight line from prominent point of forehead to prominent point of chin. This line should appear relatively vertical. Intersect a straight line along bridge of nose to prominent point of forehead and another from tip of nose to prominent point of chin.

The forehead and chin also influence how large or small the nose can appear. A slanted forehead with a receding chin creates a **convex** profile, which can give the illusion of a larger nose. A prominent forehead and chin produces a **concave** profile, which can make the nose appear smaller.

You don't have to be an artist or a mathematician to understand these principles. Becoming familiar with facial measurements not only is helpful, but in many cases is essential before you make any decision about corrective makeup or cosmetic surgery. You'll even start seeing others differently with your keener eye.

A significant part of the corrective makeup techniques that follow, and of the information in Part III ("Cosmetic Surgery—A Beauty Revolution"), is based on these preceding measurements. I know they'll help you begin the process of refining and adjusting your looks, so that you can be the best you can be and still bring out your uniqueness.

I must remind you again that although these facial measurements are very helpful, much more goes into the making of beauty than simple mathematics. Most people are not aware of their assets and focus instead on their defects. Smile the next time you look in the mirror and remember to focus on your good points. And please don't take yourself too seriously.

Part II

Makeup—It's All an Illusion

There are no ugly women;
there are only women who do not know how
to look pretty.
—JEAN DE LA BRUYERE

Cassandra Peterson ("Elvira")

*Cassandra, <u>before</u>
makeup.*

<u>*After*</u> *makeup: bigger
eyes, fuller lips,
smoother-looking skin,
and defined bone
structure.*

As "Elvira."

Chapter 2
Perfecting the Canvas

The great "cover-up"

CREATING ILLUSIONS

The photographs of my friend and client, actress Cassandra Peterson, prove a good point: *All* makeup creates an illusion. The former Las Vegas show-girl is rarely recognized when she's not made up in character.

For "Elvira," an opaque foundation transforms Cassandra's skin to an even, ghostly-white canvas, devoid of any skin undertones or imperfections. Prominent cheekbones and contours are created by using highlighter and contour shadow. Even the cleft in her chin is produced with makeup. With eyeliner, eye shadow, and artificial lashes, her pretty blue eyes become enormous and are transformed into their catlike shape.

I'm not recommending that you try to look like the "Mistress of the Dark" unless, of course, you want to. What I want you to see is that all of the steps used to create the illusion in the "Elvira" makeup demonstrate the same principles used in corrective makeup.

You've learned in chapter 1 that no one's face is mathematically symmetrical nor is anyone's skin perfectly even. In fact, a recent skin care and beauty survey has shown that the number-one makeup concern for women was camouflage. Everyone, male or female, whether black, white, Asian, Hispanic, or Mediterranean, including my clients, some of Hollywood's most beautiful celebrities, has some imperfection—a blemish, a scar, discoloration, age line, or facial feature, either temporary or permanent—that they'd like to disguise or improve.

the makeup artist's secret

The secret to great makeup is **corrective cosmetics.** They have no gender. Men as well as women can use them to conquer most "trouble" areas such as under-eye circles, scars, birthmarks, facial imbalances, and irregularities or, if they've had cosmetic surgery, post-surgical discoloration and swelling. Professionals sometimes refer to these cosmetics as "camouflage" or "para-medical" makeup.

The purpose of corrective cosmetics is to normalize or balance the skin and features, especially for women—before their everyday makeup is applied—because what you don't see is just as important as what you do see. In fact, I'm here to tell you that whenever you admire a celebrity's ability to look great without makeup, she's probably wearing corrective makeup.

Even though corrective cosmetics have been manufactured for a long time (having their origins in theatrical makeup), they've just recently become more accessible to the general public. Once only available at theatrical beauty-supply stores and specialty makeup shops, these simple and inexpensive products are starting to appear in department stores, drugstores, and salons.

THE 'THREE C'S' OF CORRECTIVE COSMETICS

Perfecting the canvas consists of three steps, which I call the "Three C's" of Corrective Cosmetics: **Counteract, Cover,** and **Create.**

Counteract corrects or balances your skin's undertone. **Cover** hides or conceals your skin's dark areas. **Create** brings out or adjusts your bone structure or features. I assure you that by incorporating my "Three C's" into your makeup routine, you'll see a professional difference. Each step contains two products that should become a part of everyone's makeup arsenal.

Not everyone needs all three steps all the time. But understanding each step will help when you need to activate your "emergency repair kit" to ensure a lifetime of perfect makeup.

Don't worry about not getting your makeup right the first time. Just wash it off and start again. Practice and have fun. You'll be amazed at how quickly you'll master my simple techniques, and they'll only add a minute or two of extra time to your current makeup routine. Using my "Three C's" in conjunction with a full beauty makeup shouldn't take you longer than twenty minutes from start to finish.

STEP 1: COUNTERACT

Correcting Redness

Product: Neutralizer

Neutralizers hide red blemishes, blotches or rashes, broken capillaries, sunburned noses, eyeglass marks, or any localized reddish areas. Sold as creams or sticks, neutralizers have a yellowish color that counteracts red without having to use foundation (a plus for men and teens) or thicker cover-ups that can turn the concealed area light pink. With normal foundations, redness sometimes creeps through during the day if neutralizers aren't used first. Since most fair-skinned people have some kind of redness (such as the area around the nostrils), neutralizers can knock out the red in these localized areas.

Application: As with all makeup, be sure that you start with a clean face (and clean hands and applicators). With your fingertip or small brush, dot a small amount of neutralizer on the red area and blend with your fingertip by lightly dabbing and smoothing into the surrounding skin.

RED BLEMISHES

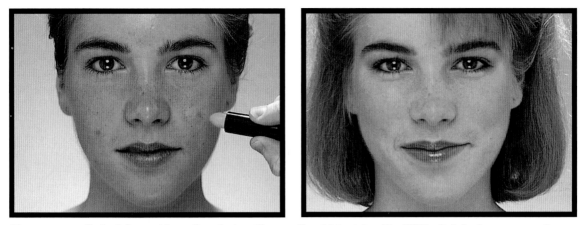

Teenagers really look best without foundation. For small red blemishes like ViVi's, lightly dot on neutralizer; then blend with fingertip or small brush; finish with a light application of eye makeup, lip color, and blusher.

You can use foundation over the neutralizer. Just be sure to pat the foundation over it with a cosmetic sponge or your fingertips.

Note: Be sure to check with your doctor first before applying any cosmetic over red, inflamed, or irritated areas. If you experience any irritation, such as itchiness, redness, or rashes, discontinue use immediately. If you notice any changes in your skin, whether or not a result of cosmetic use, it's always a good idea to consult your physician.

Correcting Undertone

Product: Color Corrector

Like neutralizers, color correctors (also called underbase color correctors, primers, or toners) don't impart color, they counteract it. Unlike neutralizers, they are an undercoat that can only be used in conjunction with a foundation (unless the color corrector is a tinted moisturizer). They're normally sold as creams or liquids and, like nor-

RED BLOTCHES

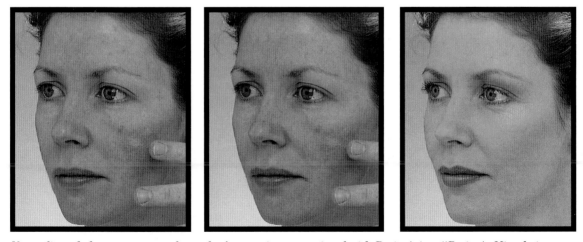

Neutralizers help counteract redness that's sometimes associated with Retin-A (see "Retin-A: Miracle in a Jar?", page 71). Notice how uniform Laura's skin becomes even though she's not wearing foundation. A light dusting of translucent face powder is all she needs before applying makeup to eyes, lips, and cheeks.

BROKEN CAPILLARIES

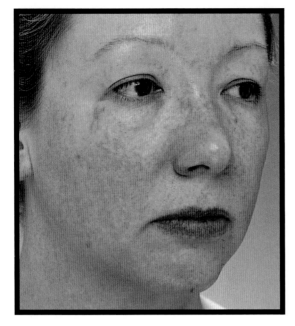

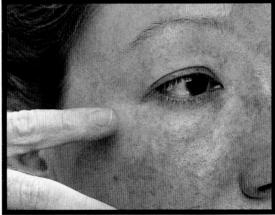

ABOVE AND ABOVE RIGHT: Judy had broken capillaries since she was three years old. She always had trouble wearing blusher because of redness. Neutralizer under normal foundation ensures an even skin tone.

RIGHT: Use neutralizer to spot-cover red areas before normal foundation. (For permanent removal of broken capillaries, see "Electrodesiccation," page 108 and "Laser Therapy," page 108.)

SALLOW SKIN

Lavender color corrector counteracts yellow-toned or sallow skin.

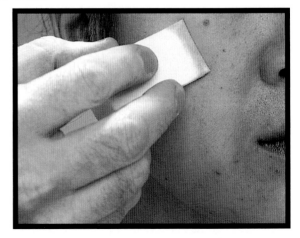

RUDDY SKIN

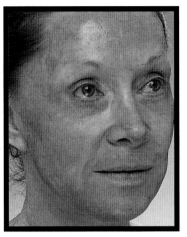

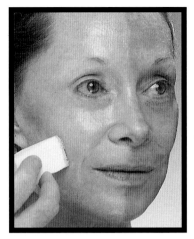

__Before__ color corrector: Similar to ruddy skin, Gwen's temporary redness from a chemical peel has taken on a fairly uniform red tone (see "Chemical Peel," page 101).

An undercoat of green color corrector counteracts red and produces a neutral, almost colorless tone.

__After__ color corrector, normal foundation, and full-color makeup: Sixty-two-year-old Gwen can now appreciate the result of her cosmetic surgery. Color corrector alleviated need for heavier foundation.

mal foundations, are light in texture. Similar to neutralizers, color correctors are based on the principle of complementary (opposite) colors (see "The Three Dimensions of Color," page 41).

If your skin has blue undertones, it appears ruddy (red) or pink. A pale green color corrector counteracts an overly red cast. If your skin has yellow undertones, it appears sallow or olive. A lavender or mauve color corrector counteracts an overly yellow cast or pallor. This doesn't mean that pink skin needs to be yellow and olive skin needs to be red. Use these products for making subtle adjustments that can add up to big improvements.

Color correctors are also helpful if your foundation changes color during the day. If you have acne or oily skin, a thin layer of color corrector will allow you to wear a sheer, water-based foundation without having to use a heavy foundation.

Application: Unlike neutralizers, color correctors are used on the entire face before normal foundation is applied. Use a wedge-shaped latex cosmetic sponge to apply a very thin coat (to avoid makeup buildup) until the yellow or red undertone disappears. Then, apply foundation with a dabbing motion with either a cosmetic sponge or your fingertips.

STEP 2 : COVER

Correcting Under-Eye Circles (and Other Shadowy Areas)

Product: Concealer

Concealers are slightly thicker and have a higher pigment content than foundations. Although primarily used around the eyes, they can also diminish shadowy areas that form depressions such as wrinkles, smile lines, or other expression lines. Don't confuse these areas with dark pigmentations such as birthmarks or age spots that require heavier coverage with camouflage cream (see "Correcting Discoloration," page 29).

To cover under-eye circles, use a concealer that matches or is just slightly lighter than your

UNDER-EYE CIRCLES

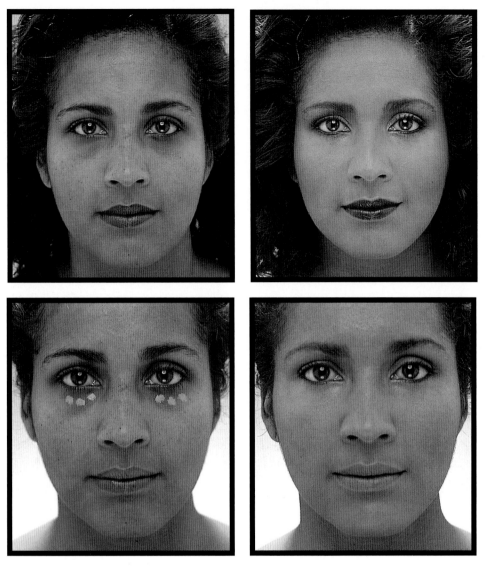

Covering Laurie's under-eye circles with concealer can make a big difference for the end result.

Concealer should be carefully blended. You never want to see concealer itself.

skin tone. For most people, concealer should contain enough yellow-to-orange pigment to block discoloration (many concealers are too pink). Otherwise it may lighten the dark area and cause a bluish or light gray color, resulting in a "racoon" look.

Concealers are sold in creams, wands, sticks, or pencils. Avoid greasy concealers. They tend to "slide off."

Men with very dark under-eye circles shouldn't feel uncomfortable using concealer. If applied sparingly, it can be undetectable and work wonders.

Application: Use your little finger or a small brush and dot a small amount of concealer onto the dark or bluish eye areas only. Don't forget any discoloration at the outer corners of the eyes. For discoloration on the upper lids, apply a small amount of concealer to the dark areas, especially the dark pockets at the inner corner of the eye (see top photographs, page 40). With your little finger, gently blend (never rub) from the inside corner out, to prevent the makeup from collecting in the fine lines. If the under-eye circle is very dark, reapply another thin layer, but avoid using too much, or "crinkling" can occur. Apply your foundation up to the concealer, feathering to smooth the edges. And yes, you can apply under-eye concealer after foundation or use it alone without foundation.

Use a concealer that is considerably lighter than your skin tone to lighten shadowy areas of the face, such as the line from the nostrils to the outside corners of the mouth (called the nasolabial fold), the line at the outside corners of the mouth (referred to as "marionette lines"), or other depressions such as pockmarks, frown lines, or the crevice on the chin just below the mouth. Soften the application with your fingertip before applying foundation (see top middle photograph, page 70).

HINT: If you have very dark circles, avoid eye shadows with cool tones such as blues or purples.

Note: For hiding under-eye bags, see "Highlighter and Contour Shadow," page 35.

Correcting Discoloration

Product: Camouflage Cream

Camouflage cream is the heart of corrective cosmetics. It covers scars, birthmarks, bruises, freckles, age spots (also called liver spots or sun spots), moles, dark patches, white patches, tattoos, spider veins, varicose veins, stretch marks, irregular lip lines, and practically any discoloration too pronounced for normal foundation or concealer to hide. Camouflage cream can also be used instead of concealer for exceptionally dark under-eye circles.

Thicker and more opaque than normal foundation and concealer, camouflage cream should be light in texture, creamy and nongreasy, as well as waterproof, perspiration-proof, smear-proof, and long-lasting.

Application: As with foundation, select a camouflage cream that most closely matches your skin color (test the color at your jawline).

Remember, your own skin color doesn't show through camouflage cream, so matching is critical to avoid a line of demarcation. It's best to check your makeup in both natural and artificial light. Rarely does one shade match your skin exactly (skin color differs on various parts of the face and body as well), but after a little practice you'll be able to quickly mix one or two shades together to make a perfect match. I promise.

With a small spatula, scoop the cream onto the back of your hand. This prevents cross-contamination (the passing of harmful microorganisms into makeup). With your fingertip, soften and blend the cream until it spreads easily.

Apply the cream to the discolored area with your fingertip with short, gentle strokes, or press with a pat-and-roll motion for more coverage. If the match isn't exact, you can always add and blend shades directly on your face. Remember, never apply camouflage cream too heavily.

If pigmentation covers the majority of your face, use a cosmetic sponge to apply a thinner coat of camouflage cream on the non-pigmented areas. As with any foundation, always use downward strokes since tiny facial hairs tend to grow downward. Be sure to blend into the hairline and just under the jawline, unless, of course, you want to cover something on your neck.

HINT: For sheerer coverage, apply camouflage cream with a dampened cosmetic sponge.

Back of hand makes a perfect palette for mixing camouflage cream.

PIGMENTATION PROBLEMS

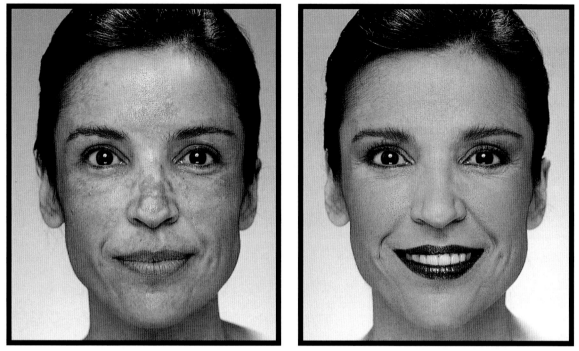

Loni's dark blotches are known as "the mask of pregnancy" or hyperpigmentation. They're caused by hormonal changes or sun damage and can be hidden with camouflage cream. Normal foundation could never do this!

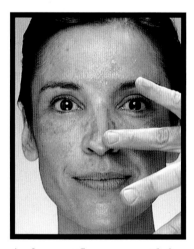

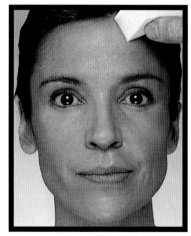

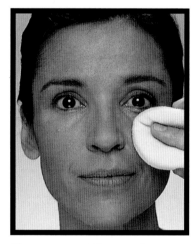

Apply camouflage cream with fingertips, using gentle, short strokes or a pat-and-roll motion.

With a sponge, spread a thinner application of camouflage cream to non-pigmented areas.

Always press setting powder over camouflage cream.

HINT: To cover large pores, stroke camouflage cream from the opposite direction to fill those that were "skipped over."

Note: For *permanent* correction of dark pigmentation, see "Chemical Peel," page 101;

"Cryosurgery," page 108; and "Laser Therapy," page 108.

Camouflage cream must be sealed with a fine milled translucent (or a shade very close to your skin tone) loose setting powder that's especially

AGE SPOTS

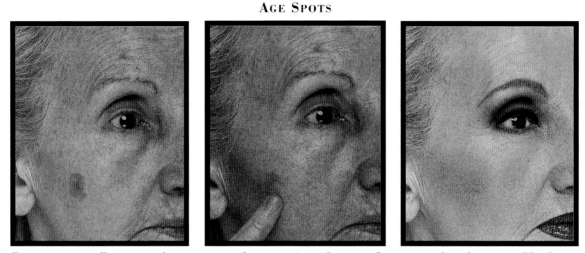

For covering small areas, such as age spots (liver spots), apply camouflage cream directly to spot. Blend into surrounding skin before applying normal foundation to entire face.

recommended for corrective makeup. It provides an extra seal to prevent it from coming off, absorbs excess oils, and reduces shine, to give skin a smoother appearance. Additionally, the powder further waterproofs the camouflage cream.

Using a cotton ball or clean cosmetic puff, dip into the powder and shake off any excess. Gently press the powder over the camouflage cream. Allow the powder to sit for at least two to three minutes, then dust off the remainder in a downward direction with a fluffy, natural-bristle powder brush. And, yes, you can use the setting powder over the rest of your face, even if it wasn't covered by camouflage cream (use powder sparingly; it can build up and "cake" by collecting in wrinkles).

HINT: For even more coverage on very dark spots, apply setting powder over first layer of camouflage cream, then add a second layer of camouflage cream, using a pat-and-roll motion.

HINT: If you've applied camouflage cream to your entire face, lightly spray face with water after you've dusted off the setting powder. Oftentimes, powder over camouflage cream creates a powdery look. The mist can add a dewy glow and help keep makeup from rubbing off.

A flat, one-dimensional look can result from using camouflage cream over the entire face. This can be remedied by shading with a darker camouflage cream to bring back depth (see "Highlighter and Contour Shadow," page 35). If surrounding skin is freckled, re-create freckles by dotting a neutral shade pencil to the camouflaged area.

The opacity of camouflage cream can also create a one-toned, "masky" look when used over the entire face. A powder blusher, applied after the setting powder, should be used to return the skin's lost tonalities. Apply the blusher to the cheeks, forehead, temples, bridge of nose, and chin, for a healthy, natural glow (see "Correcting the Cheeks," page 57).

To spot-cover sections of the face, such as age spots or a mole, simply apply the camouflage cream with your fingertip on the trouble spot— you don't have to apply it all over. You can use your normal foundation everywhere else. Feather the edges together—then finish with setting powder. Be sure the foundation matches the camouflage cream. For very tiny areas, a small-tapered, firm brush can be used to "paint out" spots (see top right photograph, page 70). You can always go back after you've applied your foundation and setting powder to spot-cover tiny areas or to retouch areas that you've missed. I call this "spot-checking."

Note: For *permanent* correction of age spots, see "Chemical Peel," page 101; "Cryosurgery," page 108; and "Laser Therapy," page 108.

If you have a large birthmark or need to cover a defined pigmentary area, start at the center of the mark and slowly work the camouflage cream outward, feathering the edges into the surrounding skin (see bottom left photograph, page 62). If you're covering a mark on only one side of your face, balance the face by using a small amount of the same colored cream on the unmarked side.

Some scars have a loss of pigment and appear white. They're easily covered by camouflage cream. Whether raised or indented, scar tissue is

INJURY SCARS

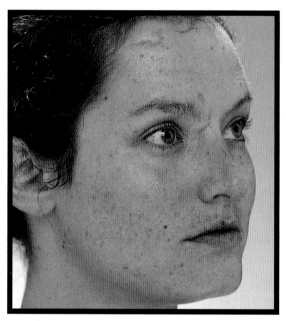

__Before__ camouflage cream: These small scars on Laurel's forehead and bridge of nose (near eyebrow) are typical injury scars.

__After__ camouflage cream, foundation, and full makeup.

For tiny areas like this, use small brushes (this is a retractable lip brush) to apply camouflage cream directly to scar; feather edges with fingertip.

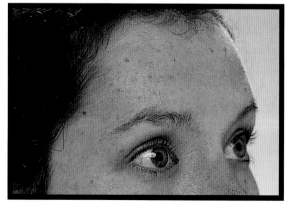

Scars can be made completely invisible by blending camouflage cream into surrounding skin.

BURN SCARS

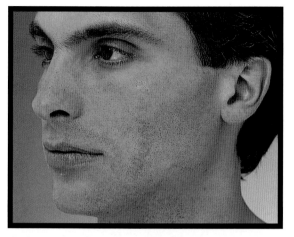

Before camouflage cream: Brent's burn scar stands out because of its location within beard area.

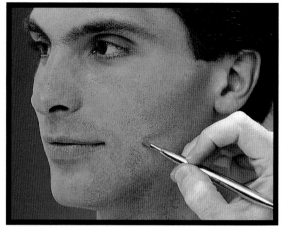

With a small brush, apply camouflage cream to scar only; then blend and seal with setting powder.

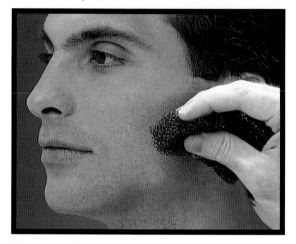

With a stipple sponge, dab charcoal-colored cream over camouflage cream to bring back stubble.

After camouflage cream and beard stipple: Brent's scar is completely camouflaged.

smooth and without pores and requires an adherent makeup, such as camouflage cream.

Before covering scars with camouflage cream, avoid using an oily moisturizer over the scar. The moisturizer can hinder adherence to scar tissue (see "Priming the Canvas," page 39).

For men, scars located within the beard area require an extra step called "stippling." After the camouflage cream and setting powder have been applied to the scar, lightly go over the scar with a stipple sponge (a textured sponge sold in theatrical beauty-supply stores and some art-supply stores) to re-create the look of stubble. First, lightly brush the sponge over a charcoal or brown

(depending on beard color) cream makeup or camouflage cream to pick up color. Blot first on the back of your hand; then lightly dab over the camouflage cream; then powder over stippled area. It's that easy!

Note: For *permanent* correction of scars, see "Permanent Makeup," page 58; "Laser Therapy," page 108; and "Scar Correction," page 109. For additional information on burns, see "Burns," pages 60-61.

We all get black-and-blue bruises once in a while. Camouflage cream is a great fix-it.

BLACK-AND-BLUE BRUISES

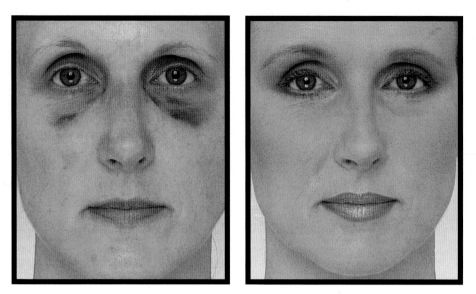

This temporary bruise is a result of nasal surgery (see "Nose Reshaping," page 110). Two layers of camouflage cream hide any trace of black-and-blue.

FRECKLES

Tracy, <u>before</u> camouflage cream.

<u>After</u> spot-covering only dark or large freckles with camouflage cream: Freckles are minimized without having to wear any foundation. For daytime makeup, Tracy retains her freckles for a fresh, outdoor look. Notice how natural her eye makeup (a color wash) and lip color (a touch of lip gloss) look as well.

<u>After</u> camouflage cream and full makeup.

I personally love freckles, but some of my clients want to cover theirs. When covering, I prefer to soften them with a sheer foundation. To completely cover freckles, you can use camouflage cream as a foundation. If you don't like to wear foundation during the day, but would like to soften your freckles, hide only the darker and larger ones by spot-covering with camouflage cream.

Note: To *permanently* lighten freckles, see "Retin-A: Miracle in a Jar?", page 71; "Alpha Hydroxy Acids," page 72; "Chemical Peel," page 101; "Cryosurgery," page 108; and "Laser Therapy," page 108.

STEP 3 : CREATE

Correcting Face Shape, Nose, Chin, and Under-Eye Bags

Product: Highlighter and Contour Shadow

Highlighter and contour shadow are probably the most fun steps of corrective makeup. Here's where you get to play artist and sculpt your face. These two products are generally used with each other. Their use exemplifies my "define" and "accent" principle of light and shadow: *Light areas appear to come forward or have prominence and dark areas seem to recede or appear smaller.* If you can remember this principle, you can become a master of highlighting and contouring, as well as a master of most makeup techniques, for that matter.

Highlighter and contour shadow can change the appearance of your face shape. Use them to widen, narrow, shorten, elongate, emphasize, or diminish various facial features. They can be an "instant diet" for a full face, diminish the appearance of a swelling on a puffy face, create angles on an undefined face, and soften angles on an angular one. You'd be surprised how many

public figures incorporate highlighting and contouring into their makeup routines. I've shown many politicians and newscasters how to correct facial imbalances with these products.

Highlighter should be approximately one to two shades lighter than your skin; and it should never be pure white in color because the white can look bluish and artificial. Contour shadow should be approximately one to two shades darker than your skin. It should look like the color of a real shadow, which is a neutral gray-brown.

I prefer highlighter and contour shadow in cream form (they can also be in pressed-powder or pencil form), so I can sculpt the face before I set with face powder. Some contouring can be accomplished with a deep-toned blusher as well (see "Correcting the Cheeks, page 57), but best results are obtained with a cream contour shadow. If you can't find professional highlighter and contour shadow, you can use a foundation that's one to two shades lighter and another that's one to two shades darker, although it might be less convenient to apply. Highlighter and contour shadow should always be used with foundation. Think of them, in fact, as a means to lighten or darken your foundation directly on your face.

Application: Apply with your fingertip, cosmetic sponge, or brush. Blend with your fingertip, using a pat-and-roll motion or dabbing with a cosmetic sponge.

HINT: This artist's trick works well when applying all makeup, but is especially helpful when using highlighter and contour shadow: Squint your eyes from time to time while applying your makeup. Like a camera's F-stop, the squinting blocks some of the light entering your eyes, decreasing extraneous detail. This enables you to see light and shadow as definite areas. You'll be amazed how much easier shading and blending become.

HINT: The steeper the angle of contour shadow under the cheekbone, the narrower the face will appear.

CREATING CHEEKBONES

<u>*Before*</u> *makeup: Even though Rebecca has a well-balanced face, highlighter and contour shadow will enhance her bone structure.*

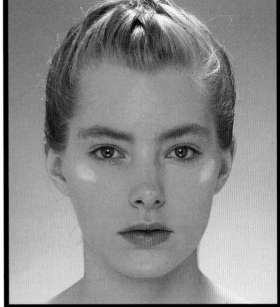

To accent cheekbones, apply highlighter on ledge of cheekbone, starting below outside corner of eye, angling diagonally toward top of ear; then blend.

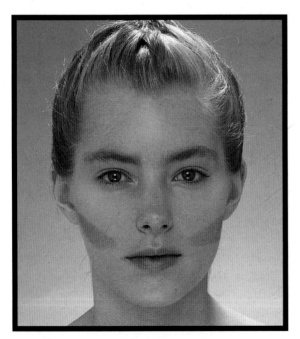

For under-cheekbone shadowing, apply contour shadow to hollow of cheek, starting at a point about mid-eye and no lower than mid-point between nose and mouth, angling diagonally toward middle of ear; then blend.

<u>*After*</u> *full makeup: Rebecca's cover-girl looks are due to higher cheekbones and a more angular face. It's critical that contour shadow be blended. You never want to see stripes of brown shadow.*

FULL FACE, DOUBLE CHIN, AND JOWLS

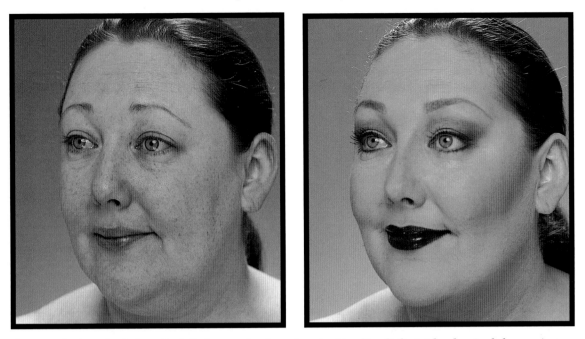

Contour shadow slenderizes Gayiel's face and reduces her double chin. It diminishes her jowls by evening out her jawline, which helps bring out her beautiful features.

Unfortunately, large women are often ignored in beauty-oriented books. Makeup for the heavier woman, particularly contour shadow, can be a valuable tool to bring the face into better balance. If you have a full face, or would like to diminish the appearance of a fleshy or double chin, jowls, an uneven jawline, or a full neck, try using contour shadow.

Generally, fleshy or full faces can be improved by bringing emphasis upward. Use makeup to "raise" the cheekbones and "lift" the eyes and eyebrows (see photographs, this page).

HINT: For a very round or wide face, apply contour from the hollow of the cheek down to the jawline.

HINT: For a prominent jaw, shade the jawline itself, blending below the jawbone.

Note: For *permanent* correction of the neck area, see "Neck Contouring," page 100.

To slenderize face, apply contour shadow under cheekbones. To narrow a wide forehead, add contour shadow to temple area. To create a more pronounced jawline, apply contour shadow directly beneath jawline; then blend. When applying contour shadow under chin, blend downward on neck until contour shadow gradually disappears. Subtlety is key.

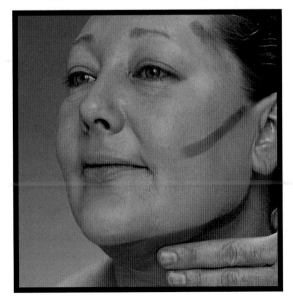

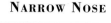

WIDE NOSE

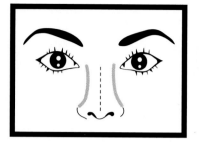

Solution: To narrow a wide nose, apply contour shadow along sides to flare of nostrils. Add highlighter to center of bridge (great for short noses); then blend. (Also see photographs, page 113.)

NARROW NOSE

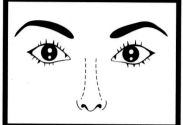

Solution: To widen nose, apply highlighter along side; then blend.

CROOKED NOSE

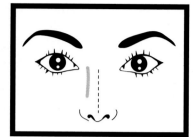

Solution: To straighten nose, apply contour shadow to crooked side and highlighter to center of bridge; then blend.

LONG NOSE

Solution: To shorten nose, apply contour shadow to base of nose; then blend.

HOOKED NOSE

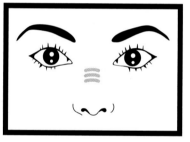

Solution: To reduce a high bridge or a bump, dot contour shadow on highest point of bump; then blend.

BAGS

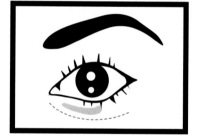

Solution: To hide bags (not discoloration), dot a tiny amount of contour shadow to center of bag (the puffiest portion), and with small-tapered brush, apply highlighter in crease directly below bag; blend by gently patting.

RECEDING CHIN

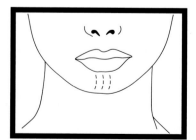

Solution: To make chin appear more prominent, apply highlighter to center of chin; then blend.

PROMINENT CHIN

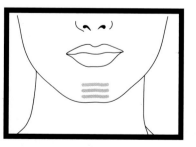

Solution: To make chin appear less pronounced, apply contour shadow to center of chin; then blend.

LONG CHIN

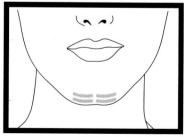

Solution: To make chin appear shorter, apply contour shadow to base of chin; then blend.

Rarely is anyone satisfied with the shape of his or her nose. Women can turn to makeup for a subtle adjustment to the nose as well as the chin by using highlighter and contour shadow.

Note: For *permanent* correction of the nose, see "Nose Reshaping," page 110. For *permanent* correction of the chin, see "Chin Augmentation," page 115.

One of the most common questions I'm asked is "How can I get rid of the bags under my eyes?" Cosmetic surgery is the only way to permanently correct them (see "Eyelid Surgery," page 89), but a simple makeup trick with highlighter and contour shadow can help if you feel you're carrying around a little too much "baggage."

Bags are raised areas. They should never be lightened, because the highlighting would call more attention to the puffiness.

Highlighting and contouring, more than almost any other corrective makeup technique, requires subtlety. Use it only for evening makeup, when light levels are lower. The importance of blending cannot be overemphasized. You should never see the makeup, only the effect. That's the true art of cosmetics.

Priming the canvas— sensible skin care

Just as corrective cosmetics help perfect your face for color makeup, priming the canvas with sensible skin care should be your first step to help perfect your skin for all makeup. The process should never be time-consuming, complicated, or expensive. Simple, sensible skin care can produce visible results if you cleanse, tone, and moisturize correctly and, it should never take longer than five minutes.

Cleansing should involve nothing more than using a non-drying, soap-free cleanser to remove every trace of makeup and any impurities on the skin surface. Splash your face repeatedly with skin-temperature water (never hot). Unless you've undergone a cosmetic procedure (see "What to Expect," page 85), are using Retin-A (see "Retin-A: Miracle in a Jar?", page 71), or have very sensitive skin, it's also a good idea to use a mild scrub (an exfoliant) a couple of times a week to slough off all dead skin cells and flakiness. This process refines and polishes the skin to produce a smoother texture for optimum application of makeup.

Toners help rid the skin of any excess surface cells, residual cleanser, makeup, or impurities. Unless your skin is extremely oily, avoid toners or astringents with alcohol, which can be drying. There's no cosmetic that can permanently reduce large pores. The effect is only temporary.

Always use a light moisturizer (and sunscreen) as a base coat prior to makeup. Aside from hydrating the skin, moisturizers plump up and smooth devitalized skin, which facilitates better adherence of makeup. They also provide smoother makeup application and better color saturation. Always apply moisturizer to dampened skin to seal in water. Wait a few minutes for the moisturizer to absorb before putting on makeup. Moisturizer should leave the skin supple, never greasy or shiny. Blot shiny areas with a tissue prior to makeup. If you have oily skin, use a light, water-based moisturizer.

Be aware that heavy eye creams can sometimes cause puffiness around the eyes. Also, to avoid streaky or smeary eye makeup, be sure to completely remove all traces of oil around the eyes before applying makeup. Unless your skin is excessively dry, avoid using any type of oil-based moisturizer on the eyelid under makeup.

Professional facials are marvelous to improve the skin, increase circulation, and reduce stress as well. Post-surgical skin care in the hands of a qualified, licensed esthetician can be an invaluable adjunct to cosmetic surgery.

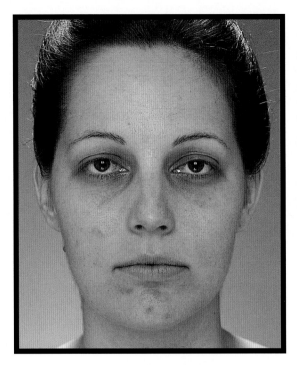

Hillary, <u>before</u> makeup.   *<u>After</u> makeup.*

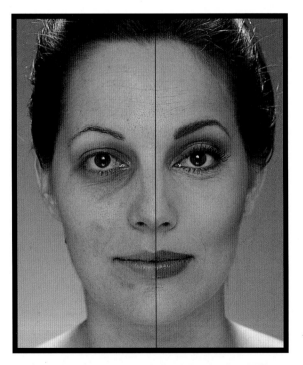

This is not a composite of two photographs that are side by side, nor has Hillary undergone cosmetic surgery. I made up just one side of Hillary's face so you could see how effectively makeup can adjust facial features. First, corrective makeup creates an even skin tone and defines bone structure; then, color makeup adjusts shape of eyes, brows, and mouth, and brings an overall healthy color to Hillary's fabulous face.

Chapter 3

Correcting Your Eyes, Brows, Lips, and Cheeks

adjusting your features with color

Now that you've learned how to perfect the canvas of your face, you're ready to adjust your features with color makeup. "Color makeup" is a general term professional makeup artists use to define cosmetics other than foundations or products used to even out your skin. It includes eye shadows, pencils, blushers, lip colors, and any other product that brings color to the face. Color makeup, if used wisely, is also corrective.

Improving your complexion and bone structure first with corrective makeup directly influences how good your eyes, brows, lips, and cheeks will look. Furthermore, these features will look even better than they've ever looked after you've learned how to professionally adjust their shape and enhance them with color makeup.

THE THREE DIMENSIONS OF COLOR

As with fine art, people often instinctively like what they see in a face without always knowing why. But just because you think a color is pretty doesn't mean it necessarily belongs on your face. You must have a basic understanding of color before you can effectively use it.

There are three dimensions of color: **Hue, Intensity,** and **Value.**

Hue identifies a color by name, such as red, yellow, or blue. Hues can be cool (blue or gray undertone) or warm (yellow or golden undertone), or a combination of both.

Intensity or saturation refers to a hue's relative brightness or dullness. The intensity of a hue can be toned down by adding its **complementary color**—its opposite color on the

THE THREE-DIMENSIONAL EYE

Just two shades of eye shadow can add dimension to any eye.

color wheel (remember Art 101?). You don't have to know every color's opposite, but some knowledge of complementary colors can help you adjust a makeup shade without having to remove it and start over (and alleviate the need to buy endless shades of makeup). These opposite colors, when mixed together, cancel each other out, creating a neutral shade that appears brownish in color (still with me?). Bright colors can also be toned down by adding beige or neutral brown.

Value is the degree of lightness or darkness of a hue. Making a color darker (or adding black) increases a color's value. Making a color lighter (or adding white) decreases its value.

By understanding the three dimensions of color, you can create the illusion of a more aesthetically pleasing and dimensional eye.

CHOOSING COLORS

Everyone, regardless of their eye color, can wear *every* color. But, it's the *particular* hue, intensity, and value of the color that determines whether or not it's flattering to you. Compare the difference between a peach color (orange with a yellow undertone) held next to your face and a coral color (orange with a pink undertone). What looks best on you is determined by your hair and eye color and your skin's undertone. It is a good idea to coordinate your eye makeup colors to your outfit, but only if you've already established that the color is complementary to your face. Generally, if you look great in earth-toned clothes, you'll look best with warm-toned makeup, and if your wardrobe consists of blues, pinks, and purples, you'll look best with cool-toned makeup.

Choosing colors for eye makeup seems to be one of the most confusing makeup decisions. If you're unsure what specific eye makeup colors are right for you or where to even begin with color, it's always safest to choose neutral muted shades. Grays, taupes, and browns are usually flattering colors for most eyes.

Be sure the color of your eye makeup doesn't overpower the color of your eyes. If you want the color of your eye itself to stand out, never match your eye shadow color with your eyes. Consider using your eye's complementary color. For example: Soft purples, pinks, and lavenders make green or hazel eyes "pop;" peaches, rusts, and browns play up blue or gray eyes; plums, charcoals, and muted greens are a great contrast for brown eyes. Regardless of your eye color, however, be careful with pink eye shadows. Pale or bright pink can make the eyes look tired.

For lining, generally browns, charcoals, and navy work best for most eye colors, with the exception of black liner, which is best for dark brunettes or exotic faces. Rarely should the color of eyeliner stand out. Again, avoid bright shades.

Correcting the eyes

The eyes truly are a reflection of the soul and an indication of one's well-being. I love making up eyes, because everyone's eyes are unique and require a different approach.

But why are most women more confused about their eye makeup than any other aspect of cosmetics? One of the reasons can be attributed to the cosmetic companies who change their eye shadow collections at least twice a year, creating an artificial need for a variety of new colors. You don't need a drawer full of multicolored eye shadows to create beautiful eyes. In fact, you'll soon see how to make up your eyes with only two shades of eye shadow!

THE THREE EYE AREAS

The eye can easily be divided into three distinct areas: the **lid,** the **crease,** and the **brow bone.** Enhancing these three areas with makeup is what brings dimension to your eyes.

LINE, DEFINE, AND ACCENT

Every eye shape can be enhanced by using my three simple steps: **Line, Define,** and **Accent.** Each eye shape, however, requires its own individual *placement* of makeup. Again, this technique is based on the theory of light and shadow. If you recall, light comes forward and dark recedes. The objective is two-fold: First, to bring dimension to the eyes; and second, to adjust their shape.

To line, define, and accent, all you need are just two eye shadows (one defining shade and one accenting shade) and one eye pencil. That's

it! I recommend you use matte pressed-powder eye shadows. Especially for daytime, stay away from obvious frosts, as most iridescent eye shadows accentuate lines and wrinkles, as well as look unnatural and harsh. Remember, we don't want to see the makeup, just the illusion.

A defining eye shadow is bolder than an accenting eye shadow. It should be darker and more muted than the accent color. An accent color can range from light to medium. The greater the difference between the define and accent colors' values (very light next to very dark) and intensities (bright next to more muted), the more dimension you create. You control a colors' values and intensities by how heavily you apply them. The size of your brush also helps determine the value and intensity you can create with a powder eye shadow. The smaller the brush, the darker the value and brighter the intensity.

EYE MAP

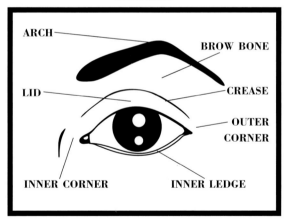

Become familiar with the areas of your eye.

Defining colors can be in the same color family as accenting colors (i.e., a brown defining color with a beige accenting color), or they can be a contrasting color (i.e., a charcoal defining color with a pink accenting color). There are no hard-and-fast rules for color selection. Just be sure the colors are flattering to you. This is an area of makeup where experimentation can truly be enjoyable.

For optimum control and ease of application, apply the defining eye shadow with a small, quarter-inch natural-bristle brush with a slanted tip (a rounded-edge brush can also be used). Use a sponge-tipped applicator (or a "fluff" brush) for applying the accenting eye shadow. Sponge-tipped applicators cover larger areas faster with less chance of eye shadow falling onto the cheek (color spill) during application. And *always* blend. What you take off is as important as what you put on.

HINT: If you wear glasses, keep them at hand to check every makeup stage. Magnifying glasses with lenses that flip up and down, allow you to see one eye at a time. They're available through catalogs or opticians.

Step 1—Line

Purpose: To bring definition to the eye shape itself, alter the size and shape of the eye, and make the eyelashes appear thicker.

Pencils are fastest and easiest to use. Just be sure they're soft, to avoid dragging or pulling the skin. An unsharpened pencil can produce too thick a line and an overly-sharpened pencil can give too harsh a line, as well as injure the skin around the eyes. To keep pencils clean, stroke the tip along a clean tissue before applying.

Black, brown-black, or navy *inner* eyeliner can create even more definition to the eye. It emphasizes and defines the outline of the eye, and can also adjust the shape of the eye (see also "Prominent Eyes," page 47). But it can also make the eye look smaller, so don't use it if you have small eyes. Conversely, a white or light inner eyeliner can help create the illusion of more white-of-the-eye to open up the eyes as well as make them appear brighter (see "Small Eyes," page 48). Light-colored inner eyeliner should never be used on the upper lid. Lining the lower lid with a dark inner eyeliner can help correct too much white-of-the-eye showing below the iris.

Application: Line the upper and lower lids along the base of the lashes, but slightly widen the line from the inner corner to the outer corner of the eye. For most eyes, starting the line on the lower lid about one third of the way from the inner corner helps make the eyes appear larger and more elongated. If the line appears too hard or dark, then soften with a small brush or sponge-tipped applicator, cotton swab, or cosmetic sponge.

Some people tend to have problems with their eyeliner creeping (smearing) or staying on. Try using a cake eyeliner instead. Lining with a matte eye shadow is another good alternative. Use a tiny, one-sixteenth-inch, short-tapered, natural-bristle brush. Moisten the brush first with water before applying the shadow.

Liquid eyeliners create a more obvious line, so avoid them unless you want a harder line.

To apply inner eyeliner to the bottom lid, gently lower your lid with your fingertip and carefully stroke a soft, blunt pencil along the entire inner ledge above the lashes. For upper lids, gently lift your lid with your fingertip and carefully apply liner along the entire rim under the lashes. Avoid inner eyeliner if you wear contacts.

HINT: To keep pencil eyeliner from smearing and lock in color, with a small brush, go over the penciled line with a matching shade of eye shadow.

HINT: If you want to bring out the color of your eyes, use inner eyeliner on the lower lid that matches the color of your iris (or slightly brighter): i.e., for blue eyes to appear even bluer, apply light blue inner eyeliner to lower lid only. This trick acts as a mirrored reflection of your eyes (see top photographs, page 88). Using light blue is also great for bloodshot eyes to give the illusion of "whiter whites."

Note: For *permanent* eyeliner, see "Permanent Makeup," page 58.

LINE: *From inner to outer corner, line upper and lower lid along lash line (start narrow at inner corner and gradually widen to outer corner); then lightly smudge.*

Step 2—Define

Purpose: To bring out or establish depth and contour to the eye area, diminish prominence, or reduce puffy eyelids, and hide wrinkled or "crepey" skin around the lid.

I prefer to use the defining eye shadow before the accenting eye shadow because it establishes the eye shape first.

Application: First, tap the brush or blow off excess powder; then lightly stroke the brush across the back of your hand as a blotter. This prevents depositing too much color, potential streaking, or the possibility of color spill (flecks on your cheek). Instead of applying eye shadow in the crease of a closed eye, keep the eye open to make a fake crease above the real crease. This will create a larger, more deep-set eye. Keeping the eye open will allow you to follow the natural contour of the eye to achieve the best shape. Using light, short strokes, apply the defining eye shadow to the crease, starting at the outer corner of your eye. Work inward to the inner corner, darkening the crease *and* the area slightly above it, going about halfway up to the brow (an overly light brow bone can appear puffy). Go back with the defining shadow, and in the form of a triangle pointing outward and upward, darken the outer third of the lid (up to the newly darkened crease you just created). Be sure to extend the shadow diagonally, but fade out gradually to where the eyebrow ends (see "Correcting the Brows," page 50). Blend and soften either with your fingertip, small-rounded brush, sponge-tipped applicator, or cosmetic sponge.

DEFINE: *Apply defining color along (and inside) crease, as well as to area above (about halfway from crease to brow). Add defining color to outer third of lid (this should be darkest area), extending outward and upward; then blend.*

ACCENT: *Apply accent color on lid and brow bone, overlapping into defining color; then blend.*

HINT: Always lightly powder the eyelids before eye shadow, for "slide" (smoother application). Also, using a pale, matte eye shadow first can act as a base and produce a more even color.

HINT: If lids are crepey, use an eye base first to prevent color from creasing.

Note: If your lid is fleshy or puffy, your natural crease may not be evident. Feel the bone with your finger to locate its placement. Apply the defining color just beneath the bone.

Step 3—Accent

Purpose: To lighten any areas that need to be pronounced or come forward.

Application: With a sponge-tipped applicator apply accenting eye shadow over entire lid and brow bone. Use the back of your hand as a blotter first. You can always add more for greater intensity and value. Blend either with your fingertip, brush, cotton swab, sponge-tipped applicator, or cosmetic sponge.

Note: An accent can also be achieved by applying a slightly pearlized, light color eye shadow (usually ivory, beige, pink, or peach).

Note: Be sure to deftly blend both the accenting and defining colors. Avoid an obvious triangle at the outer corner of the eye and any hard edges or lines of demarcation.

FINDING YOUR EYE TYPE

Find your eye type or combination of eye types from the following examples. Use the corresponding corrective technique to adjust the shape of your eyes. I've intentionally shown you how the specific areas for lining, defining, and accenting look *before* blending.

Note: The eyebrows play an important role in adjusting the eyes (see "Correcting the Brows," page 50).

CLOSE-SET EYES

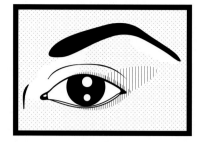

CHARACTERISTIC: *Less than one eye-length apart.*
GOAL: *To make eyes appear farther apart.*
CORRECTIVE TECHNIQUE:
　Line only outer half of upper and lower lid and extend outward to give illusion of eyes being farther set.
　Define outer third of eye and extend outward to elongate eye area.
　Accent inner corner of eye to give illusion of more space between eyes; accent outer portion of brow bone to draw attention outward.
　Brows: Create more space between brows; extend outer end of brows to give illusion of farther-apart eyes and entire eye area appearing extended.

WIDE-SET EYES

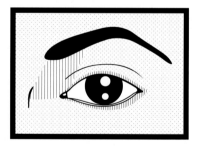

CHARACTERISTIC: *More than one eye-length apart.*
GOAL: *To make eyes appear closer together.*
CORRECTIVE TECHNIQUE:
　Line entire eye to create emphasis.
　Define inner corner of eye, blending from sides of nose to beginning of brow to bring focus inward to give illusion of eyes being closer together.
　Accent outer two-thirds of eye and brow bone with a light to medium shade to de-emphasize wide-set appearance.
　Brows: Create less space between brows to give illusion of eyes appearing closer together.

PROMINENT EYES

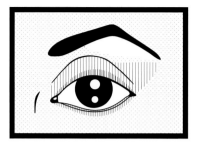

CHARACTERISTIC: *Lids appear to protrude and eyes may seem to bulge.*

GOAL: *To diminish prominence of lid area.*

CORRECTIVE TECHNIQUE:

Line entire eye to emphasize eye shape to play down lid; apply dark inner eyeliner to inner ledge of lower lid to give illusion of less white-of-the-eye.

Define entire lid with a dark or muted matte color to help hide prominence; extend outer corner of eye to elongate rounded lid.

Accent brow bone to take focus away from lid.

Brows: Sharpen arch of brows to counteract roundness of lid area.

ROUND EYES

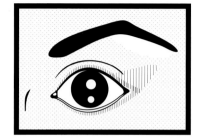

CHARACTERISTIC: *Eyes appear round.*

GOAL: *To make eyes appear more elongated.*

CORRECTIVE TECHNIQUE:

Line entire eye, extending line outward at outer corner to create an elongated eye.

Define outer corner of eye, extending outward to elongate.

Accent outer portion of brow bone to elongate brow bone area.

Brows: Extend brows to elongate eye; create a sharper arch to reduce round appearance of eye.

DEEP-SET EYES

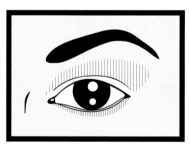

CHARACTERISTIC: *Eyes appear recessed or shadowed by prominent brow bone (lids may be hidden); often brows appear low.*

GOAL: *To make eyes appear more open and less deep-set.*

CORRECTIVE TECHNIQUE:

Line lower lid to emphasize since upper lid is hidden, lining upper lid could create a more sunken look.

Define area just above (but not in) crease and almost to brow to diminish prominent brow bone.

Accent entire lid to bring it forward.

Brows: If brows are low, raise them to create more height; darken light brows (pale brows with deep-set eyes can make eyes appear even more deep-set).

DOWN-SLANTING EYES

CHARACTERISTIC: *Eyes droop downward at outer corners.*

GOAL: *To make eyes appear to angle upward.*

CORRECTIVE TECHNIQUE:

Line upper lid angling upward at outer corner to lift; line lower lid with line fullest at mid-point and angling upward at outer corner of eye to de-emphasize droop.

Define outer corner of eye, angling upward to lift.

Accent highest point of brow bone to bring focus upward from eye itself.

Brows: Raise outer end of brows to create illusion of droop being lifted.

HOODED EYES

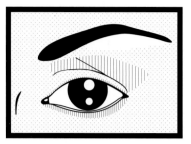

CHARACTERISTIC: *Fold of skin covers outer area of eyelid like an overhang (characteristic of aging).*
GOAL: *To diminish effect of hood.*
CORRECTIVE TECHNIQUE:

Line entire eye but keep line close to lash line on upper lid to emphasize eye's shape.
Define hood itself above crease at outer corner of eye to diminish hood.
Accent highest point of brow bone to make it appear higher.
Brows: Raise outer end of brows to create illusion of hood being lifted.

Note: For *permanent* correction of hooded eyes, see "Eyelid Surgery," page 89; and "Forehead-Lift," page 97.

SMALL EYES

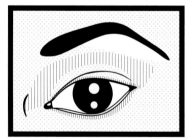

CHARACTERISTIC: *Eyes seem overpowered by other features.*
GOAL: *To make eyes appear larger.*
CORRECTIVE TECHNIQUE:

Line entire eye with a light to medium shade to avoid closing it in; apply a light shade of inner eyeliner to inner ledge of lower lid to give illusion of adding more white-of-the-eye.
Define crease and outer corner of eye to emphasize and elongate.
Accent lid and brow bone to make them seem larger.
Brows: Extend brows to make entire eye area appear larger.

Note: Glasses for farsightedness magnify and accentuate eye makeup. If you wear glasses for farsightedness, be sure to keep your eye makeup very subtle. For nearsightedness, play up your eyes since the lenses can make them appear smaller.

ORIENTAL EYES

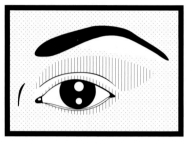

CHARACTERISTIC: *Almond-shaped with little or no crease (fold of skin may cover lid); flat brow bone.*
GOAL: *To add depth and dimension by creating distinction between lid, crease, and brow bone (but still retain eye's inherent ethnic characteristic).*
CORRECTIVE TECHNIQUE:

Line entire eye but keep line close to lash line on upper lid to avoid fold of skin.
Define inner corner of eye near sides of nose, blending along side of bridge, to create more dimension; continue line into crease area of eye (mid-point between upper lash line and brow) to simulate crease.
Accent brow bone to make it more prominent (to further help divide eye area into three parts).
Brows: Extend brows if eyes are small to make eye area seem larger.

Note: To *permanently* create an eyelid crease, see "Eyelid Surgery," page 89.

You've now learned the professional way of bringing dimension and shape to your eyes. You don't have to be an artist to use these techniques. Keep practicing. And trust your common sense. Also, the order in which you use my techniques is not etched in stone. You might feel better applying your accent color first and lining last. My main concern is that you achieve the most satisfying results in the easiest way. That's what professionals do. I know you'll feel like a professional in no time.

BIG TO BIGGER: MASCARA

Did you know that longer lashes make the face look younger? If I were to choose one makeup product to enhance the face, my choice would be mascara. Mascara not only darkens, lengthens, and thickens the lashes, but it also functions as a corrective measure to intensify the depth of the eye, making it appear larger.

Most people's lashes naturally grow downward. Mascara can exaggerate this and even close the eye in. My favorite remedy is to use an eyelash curler *before* mascara. It coaxes the lashes upward to help open the eyes. Avoid curling your lashes after applying mascara to prevent it from cracking and flaking. Also, the curler can pull out the lashes after the mascara has been applied.

To use the curler effectively, you should bend the lashes at three different points, rather than crimp in one spot, to create a definite curve. Gently close the curler with a tight pressure (never pulling) at the base of the lashes; hold for about ten seconds (making sure all lashes are inside curler); release and crimp again in the middle of the lashes; hold again for another ten seconds; then repeat the process a third time at the ends of the lashes.

Most often, I use black mascara on everyone. If applied properly, it can work fine for the fairest of faces (even for daytime). I sometimes use brown or dark brown on blondes or redheads, depending on the intensity of the eye makeup. Sometimes I use brown mascara for the lower lashes and black for the upper, or I omit mascara entirely on the lower lashes, keeping them bare. You can be the best judge of color. Just remember, for more definition, intensity, or drama, go darker. Although some of the newer colored mascaras (purples, blues, greens, etc.) have their place, I don't feel they offer enough corrective value.

Application: Apply mascara sparingly to the lower lashes first to avoid smearing from the upper lashes onto the brow bone area. To avoid clumps, wipe the mascara wand with a tissue before starting; then, holding the wand vertically, lightly brush across the lashes with the tip of the wand. Immediately separate with a lash comb (the metal-pronged comb is best), or small brush to eliminate clumps or a spiky look.

For upper lashes, first use the tip of the wand and stroke downward on the top of each lash then up on the underside. It's important to coat the base of the lashes near the root (especially for blonds with light lashes) to create more density for a thicker-looking lash line. Then, hold the wand horizontally, and from underneath the lash, flick upward. Wiggling the wand can help spread the color and separate the lashes. Separate with a lash comb or brush. When dry, add another coat or two for thicker-looking lashes. Always allow the mascara to dry between coats to avoid clumps and an overdone, artificial look.

If you have exceptionally long lashes (everyone should have this problem!), mascara could create a peculiar "spidery" look. Apply mascara with the tip of the wand at the roots of the lashes only. If you have very sensitive eyes, opt for cake mascara moistened with water (never saliva).

HINT: For even longer lashes, use a small brush to dust the lashes with a little loose powder between coats.

HINT: For tired, droopy, or down-slanting eyes, apply additional mascara only to the outer corner of upper lashes to create a slightly winged effect that will lift the eye.

HINT: Having your lashes professionally dyed ("lash tint") not only darkens your lashes for up to six weeks, but can actually thicken them as well.

HINT: An eyelash perm (available at many salons) will curl your lashes and last for six to eight weeks, alleviating the need to use an eyelash curler.

BIGGER TO BIGGEST: ARTIFICIAL LASHES

Dietrich used them. Sophia still wears them. Liza and Madonna love them. Lucy, Goldie, and Twiggy were never photographed without them. And, guess what? They're back! But in a more natural way. Even today's youngest models are incorporating false lashes into their eye makeup.

False eyelashes make any eyes appear bigger. They can even alter the shape of the face. They must never, however, detract from or overpower your makeup. If you have sparse lashes, or simply want to embellish what you have, false lashes can do the trick (see photographs, page 52). And if you haven't any lashes at all, they can work wonders (see top left and bottom photographs, page 59). The best news about today's lashes is that they don't have to look false. Most brands come with simple directions and the rubber-cement adhesive that's easy to use and easy to remove. They come in strips, individuals, or clusters (the shorter versions are best), and can be bought almost anywhere makeup is sold. Many of the least expensive lashes look great. Oprah Winfrey, who always wears false lashes, told me her favorites are from the five-and-dime.

Application: All artificial lashes should be put on after your mascara has dried. The clusters are easiest to apply. Apply clear eyelash glue to the tip of the cluster. Using a tweezers, nestle the cluster next to your real lashes at the outside corner, fixing into place with slight pressure. For fuller overall lashes, place additional clusters along your lash line.

Individual lashes are applied in a similar fashion. Place them between your real lashes for a lush effect. Use three lashes positioned at the outer corner. Then, I evenly space three more from the center of the eye to the outer three. This creates a natural winged effect that lifts the outer corner, which is especially effective for down-slanting eyes. Both the cluster and individual lashes are secured with a dab of eyelash glue at the end and attached to your own lash.

For strip lashes, measure the strip to your lash line. Cut the strip a fraction shorter than your lash line so you can place it slightly within the inner corner of the eye.

Before applying, trim the length of the hairs with manicuring scissors so they'll look more natural. Be sure to trim the hairs at the end of the strip shorter than at the center. Never cut them straight across. Feather the edges by cutting into the tips to form an irregular line so that some hairs are shorter than others, like your own natural lashes. Add eyelash glue to the band with a clean toothpick or pin (this prevents applying too much glue). Hold strip in a horseshoe shape for a few seconds (to allow adhesive to get tacky), then gently place the strip as close as possible to your natural lash line. Press gently in the center, before positioning both ends. Go back with eyeliner to fill in gaps between the strip and your natural lash line. Add additional mascara to the natural and false lashes to fuse them together.

Correcting the brows

"I never know what to do with my eyebrows, so I just leave them alone." I hear this all the time from my clients.

Even though the eyebrows are one of the most visible facial features, I'm always surprised at the number of women I meet who completely ignore them. The eyebrows act as a frame for the eyes and even help dictate the placement of eye makeup. In fact, your entire facial harmony is affected by the brows, particularly because emotion is expressed with their movement. Even the way the nose is perceived is influenced by the brows. So, please don't ignore them.

In the twentieth century, styles of eyebrows have rapidly changed, reflecting the stimulating growth of the times, from the highly arched, drawn-on, thin brows of the twenties to the fuller and natural-looking groomed brows of the

THE WELL-BALANCED BROW

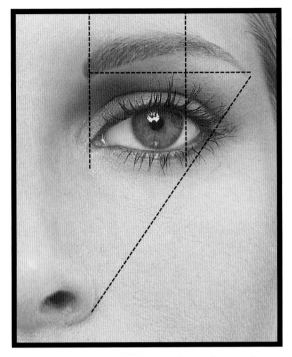

Use this diagram to help you make eyebrow adjustments.

nineties. Even though fashion is constantly changing, it's more important to first consider what the most appropriate eyebrow is for *you*.

THE FIVE CHARACTERISTICS OF BROWS

You can determine if your brows are right for your face by understanding their correlation to your eyes. The look of your brow is determined by these five characteristics: **Balance, Height, Thickness, Shape,** and **Color.**

Balance: Hold a pencil (or makeup brush) vertically from the inside corner of your eye directly up to your brow. The brow should begin at this point or just slightly closer to the bridge of the nose. The arch (the highest point) should be situated just beyond the outer edge of the iris (the colored portion). Next, hold the pencil diagonally from the outside corner of your nostril past the outer corner of your eye and up to the brow

area. This is where the brow should end. The outer end of the brow should be no lower or higher than where the brow begins.

If the brows are short, ending after the arch, the eye appears incomplete. Brows extending straight out or angling upward can create a sinister look. Down-slanting brows often create a sad look. Balancing the brow's angle can also be improved by adjusting the brow's height.

Height: The space between the eyes and the highest point of the brows should be approximately equal to the size of the iris. The larger the space, the easier it is to create big eyes with makeup. Brows that are too high, though, cannot only make the eyes appear too small, but can give the face a surprised look. Brows that are too low can make the face appear angry and are

To lift down-slanting brows (top), completely tweeze away all hair from arch outward (middle), then draw in new shape angling upward (bottom). In this case, height between eye and beginning of brow (which is naturally high) was retained, but thickness, shape, and color were adjusted.

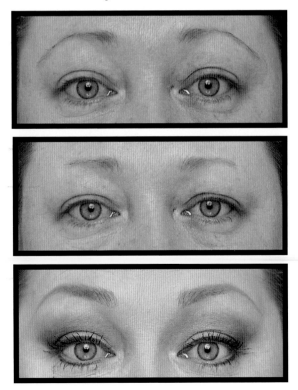

aging. If one of the brows is higher than the other, the result may be an imbalanced-looking face (see top photographs, page 86).

Thickness: The bone structure of the face helps determine the brow thickness. Full brows, which make men's eyes appear larger and more pronounced, can have the opposite effect with women. Full brows on women can appear heavy, overpower the eyes, and actually make the eyes look smaller. And since very full brows are more masculine, they're not always the most complementary for women with strong features (see top photographs, page 56) or aging faces (see top photographs, page 86).

Thinner brows are more feminine, and have a softening effect. If the brows are too thin, though they can look artificial, giving the face a cold, less youthful or dated appearance (see top photographs, page 40).

To make brows fuller, draw in brows either from below or above, depending upon how much height is needed.

Brushing up the brows can also create a more youthful look and wide-eyed effect.

Shape: The brows should taper, being the fullest above the inner corner of the eye and should never be drawn with a hard edge or be uniform in density (see top photographs, page 40). Brows with a high arch create more space (see **Height,** page 51) between the eye and brow. This is a more feminine characteristic. Brows

that are closer together (see **Balance,** page 51) are considered more masculine. Men's brows, which are usually horizontal, can also appear feminine if they taper too much.

To separate close-together brows, tweeze between the brows. For brows that are too far apart, draw in tiny hairs at the beginning of each brow.

Color: Generally, brows should be the same color as your hair or a shade lighter. For very light or gray hair, brows should be a shade or two darker than the hair color. If brows are too dark, professional lightening can do wonders for the face. When changing hair color, adjusting the brow color should always be considered. This should be done by a professional hair colorist.

Neutral, matte eye shadows are best for emphasizing brows. For nonexistent or sparse brows use two shades of pencil (combine the pencils with the matte eye shadow) to simulate hair: taupe and brown for blondes, brown and gray for brunettes. For black hair, use charcoal, which is more natural looking. And please remember, the darker the brow, the more focus it pulls.

Application: Lana Turner, the eternally beautiful screen legend, once told me that "a steady hand and a firm brush" is all that's necessary for drawing on natural-looking eyebrows. I can't give better advice than that.

To re-create realistic eyebrows when there are none, use a firm, slant-tipped brush with matte eye shadow (or "brush-on-brow") to establish brow shape. Next, with a well-sharpened pencil sketch in short, diagonal, feathery strokes to simulate hair; then powder to reduce shine and make it last. Brush brows upward with a brow brush (or clean, stiff toothbrush) to blend. An obvious, one-toned, penciled-in look should always be avoided.

HINT: To darken pale brows, use mascara (usually brown). Blot wand with a tissue, then lightly brush brows upward.

HINT: For stubborn or unruly brows, or for keeping the hairs brushed upward, use a brow-setting product, hair spray, or sculpting gel on a brow brush or clean, stiff toothbrush, and comb upward. (Avoid getting these products in or near the eyes.)

GROOMING THE BROWS

Before makeup, tweezing can be one of the most important corrective steps. Slanted-edge tweezers are easiest to use (be sure tweezers are always clean). An antiseptic should be used on the skin before and after tweezing. Generally, pluck the hair from *under* your natural brow line and always in the direction of growth. But if brows are overly arched or too high, carefully tweeze from above and draw in below. Remove all stray hairs from below the brows to ensure a clean brow bone area. Pluck stray hairs between the brows and near the temple. Avoid over-tweezing, since brow hairs don't always grow back.

Having brows professionally waxed can be a marvelous solution for reshaping. Since waxing removes hair from below the skin's surface, regrowth becomes less frequent (about one month), and with repeated waxing, regrowth eventually becomes sparser. You might also want to consider permanent removal by electrolysis (also see "Unwanted Hair on the Upper Lip," page 57).

Soft, full brows are more attractive and contemporary looking than long, bushy brows, which can look unruly and unkempt. The best way to trim the brows is to first brush them upward with a brow comb, carefully trim the hairs with small manicure scissors (don't snip them too short or create an obvious straight line), and then brush the brows upward into place.

Note: For *permanent* brows and eyeliner, see "Permanent Makeup," page 58.

Correcting the lips

After eyes, most people notice the lips next. Since I reserve applying lip makeup until the end, it still always amazes me how much the lips can affect the appearance of the entire face. Even if the lips are well balanced with the rest of the features, adjusting their shape and creating definition with lip lining before adding color is an important function of lip makeup.

LINING THE LIPS

Lining with a lip pencil is the easiest way to shape your lips. It accomplishes two things: It defines the lips and also acts as a boundary for the lip color by keeping it from "feathering" (lip color that "bleeds" into the tiny vertical lines around the lips). Powdering over the pencil line before adding lip color also helps keep the color in place.

Lip pencils should be approximately the same as, or slightly darker than, the lip color (and always in the same color family). You never want to see an obvious outline. You should have at least three pencils on hand: a warm-toned rust-colored pencil for warm-toned lip colors (rusts, peaches, browns, etc.), a pink-toned pencil for cool-toned lip colors (pinks, mauves, purples, etc.), and a red pencil for red lip color (blue-red or orange-red). For dark skin, opt for darker variations of the color pencils I've suggested.

Application: Before lining, use a lip conditioner (or lip primer to prevent feathering), which fills in tiny lines to help smooth the lips and permits lip color to glide on more easily. Then apply foundation directly to the lips. This ensures truer and more even color, helps the lip color stay on

EASY SOLUTIONS TO LIP PROBLEMS

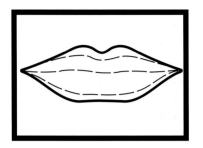

THIN LIPS

Solution: With lip pencil, outline lips outside natural lip line. Extend slightly above bow of upper lip and slightly below center of lower lip. Avoid dark or bright colors. Highlight center of lower lip (to *permanently* make lips fuller, see "Fuller Lips with Collagen," page 106).

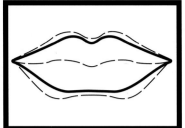

TOO FULL LIPS

Solution: First hide natural lip line with camouflage cream (or concealer). Then, with lip pencil, outline lips inside natural lip line. Avoid dark or bright colors, or over-glossing.

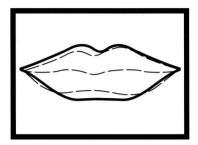

UNEVEN LIPS

Solution: For irregularly shaped lips, make both sides of lips match by lining preferred side, then mimic shape on opposite side. If lower lip is fuller, outline lips inside lower lip and line outside upper lip. Use darker shade on lower lip. If upper lip is fuller, outline upper lip inside and line lower lip outside. Use darker shade on upper lip.

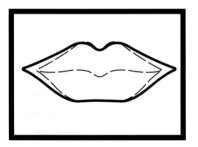

SHORT MOUTH

Solution: With lip pencil, extend lip line beyond outer corners of mouth.

LONG MOUTH

Solution: Camouflage corners of mouth. Then, with lip pencil, start lip line within inside corners of mouth (be sure corners are slightly upturned to avoid a downward droop). If lips are also thin, increase height of center of upper lip by outlining slightly above bow, and increase fullness of lower lip by outlining slightly below center.

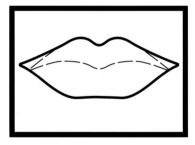

DOWN-SLANTING MOUTH

Solution: With lip pencil, raise lip line at outer corners of mouth. Use lighter shade of lip color at outer corners of lips and darker shade in center.

longer, and is another way to prevent feathering. Then set with face powder.

I'm always surprised when I see women trying to line their mouth with their lips apart. Lining with the lips together is the only logical way of accurately seeing how to adjust their shape. With a well-sharpened (but not too sharp) pencil, start lining at the center of the upper lip. Notice the two highest peaks that form the bow (or cupid's bow) of the lip. From each peak, follow the natural outline of the border of the lip, and draw a line to the outside corners of the mouth. Connect the peak to form the "V" (called the "crest") of the upper lip. Be sure, however, to avoid obvious, hard-edged peaks. Next, find a point at the center of the natural outline of the lower lip and draw a line to the outside corners of the mouth. Now, part the lips to be sure the line connects at the corners. Smudge the line a bit with your finger or cosmetic sponge and set with face powder.

Note: For *permanent* lining of the lips, see "Permanent Makeup," page 58.

ENHANCING THE LIPS WITH COLOR

The most important point to remember about lip color is that it should be flattering to you and compatible with the rest of your makeup. Coordinating lip color to your outfit is secondary. Of course, if your outfit has a predominant color, such as a purple dress, choosing an orange shade of lip color would be inappropriate.

Lip color is usually the culprit that targets someone as being too made up. And it's usually a result of the color being too dark or too bright. Darker colors and brighter colors exaggerate. For instance, using a dark or bright shade on full lips would make the lips seem even fuller, and using a dark or bright shade on thin lips would make thin lips seem even thinner.

By the way, going darker and brighter is usu-

ally all that's necessary to change a daytime lip makeup to an evening makeup.

I realize that many women initially feel a little uncomfortable going outside their natural lip line to achieve fuller lips. Again, this only becomes obvious if the lip color is too dark or bright, which calls attention to the makeup itself. You'd be amazed how much fuller your lips can still become by skillfully lining outside the lip line, then following with a soft pale shade (see top photographs, page 88).

Lip color itself has another factor: *finish* (or shine). Lip color ranges from glossy to matte to frosted. Glossy (or anything reflective) calls attention to itself. Mattes can be more subtle, and because of their formulation, they stay on longer and are less likely to feather. For a moist-looking mouth, opt for a transparent lip color rather than over-glossed lips. Subtle frosts can add luminescence and even make the lips appear fuller but overdoing can look cheap.

Application: Use a square-tipped lip brush with short, firm, sable bristles to apply the color. The precision of the brush allows for more control than when using a lipstick directly. Retractable lip brushes, sold in most beauty supply stores and drugstores, are nice to work with and less messy for easy carrying. Stroke the lip brush across the sides of the lipstick (this allows your lipstick to retain its shape), and with the lips slightly parted, apply the color to the center of the lower lip. Spread the color to the corners of the mouth and fill in the outlined lips. Extend just to the outline, but not over it. Blotting isn't necessary after lip color. Why remove color that's just been applied? If you prefer less color, gently *pat* the lips with a tissue.

HINT: For that perfect shade, mix lip colors directly on lips. You'll be amazed by how many colors you'll create.

HINT: For a "stained" and less saturated look, color in entire lip with a lip pencil only.

FACIAL HAIR ON UPPER LIP

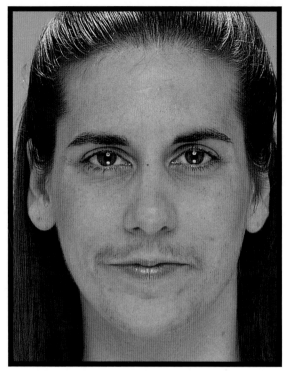

Alexandra (age 36), <u>before</u> electrolysis.

<u>After</u> electrolysis and makeup: Alexandra's overall look appears much more feminine with the addition of eyebrow tweezing.

"I started to develop excess facial hair at eleven. Makeup only called attention to the problem. I only wish I would have started electrolysis earlier. It took less than two years to complete and was relatively painless. Even though the center of my upper lip was a little sensitive, the benefits outweighed the inconvenience."

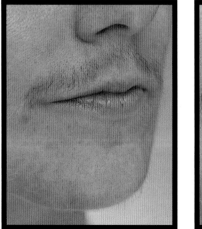

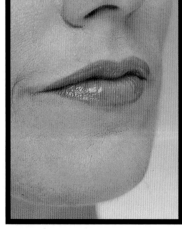

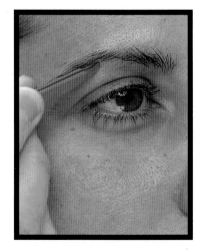

After unwanted hair is removed above lip, Alexandra's mouth appears much prettier. A smoother upper lip ensures a crisper, less messy lip line.

Alexandra's overall look can be further softened by tweezing her brows.

HINT: For a very matte look, blot lips after applying lip color; then lightly powder over color.

HINT: For lip color that lasts and lasts, fill in lips with lip pencil; powder lips; apply lip color; powder again; add another layer of color.

HINT: For non-messy powdering, place a single-ply tissue over lips and apply powder over tissue.

HINT: To give lips that sexy pout, highlight center of lower lip to make the lip seemed "rolled" by blending a white or lighter shade of lip color directly over existing color.

Lip gloss or petroleum jelly adds shine. Remember that a shinier mouth will draw more attention to the lips. But, avoid an over-glossed mouth as it can appear greasy and actually cheapen makeup. For a moist look, lightly blot your lip color with a tissue before adding a touch of gloss. For a translucent look, apply gloss *before* lip color. Or, to just add a subtle glisten, apply gloss only to the center of the lower lip.

UNWANTED HAIR ON THE UPPER LIP

Since the purpose of lining the lips is to define them and create a crisp line, facial hair above the upper lip can cause the line to appear uneven and call attention to the facial hair itself.

Bleaching the hair above the upper lip (a process that lasts about a month) might bring less attention to the hair itself, but it can't achieve a perfectly smooth lip line and is never really a solution. And, because facial hair can appear even more obvious after foundation, it's still very difficult to create a clean lip line.

For the smoothest, most attractive lip line, I recommend "de-fuzzing" with a depilatory, or even better, a professional lip waxing. Both last about a month. Depilatories are chemical hair dissolvers which can be used at home, but should always be preceded with a patch test for safety. Electrolysis is the only medically proven method for *permanent* hair removal. Be sure to find a licensed electrologist who is registered in your state. The initials R.E. (registered electrologist) signify this. Ask your dermatologist for a recommendation.

Note: Avoid depilatory products when using Retin-A (see "Retin-A: Miracle in a Jar?", page 71).

Balance between the lips and eyes is essential for tasteful makeup. Generally, if you play up the eyes, opt for a light colored, neutral, or less bright lip color. If your lips are your best feature, choose a darker or brighter color and use minimal eye makeup. This rule not only allows bringing focus to one's best feature, but generally ensures that the makeup will not look overdone.

Correcting the cheeks

Most women are confused about where to apply blusher. Generally, blusher should start at a point no lower than the bottom of the nose and no farther in than the center of the iris (the colored portion) of the eye. Blusher should angle upward toward the top portion of the ear and should be blended carefully to the hairline. Avoid bringing blusher too close to the eye—it can close up the eye.

For a long or narrow face, never apply blusher too high on the face or too close in toward the nose. Keep the color low and horizontal on the cheek. For round, wide, or square faces, bring the blusher closer toward the nose, blending upward and outward. Usually, the best color blusher for you is the one that's closest in color to your natural blush. Most women can choose from peaches, pinks, and corals. Reds and mahoganies are best for darker, black, or olive skin.

Powder blusher is the easiest to use. It should

be applied after foundation or camouflage cream has been sealed with setting powder. Cream blusher is better for wrinkled cheeks and it should be applied before the setting powder.

Application: Apply powder blusher with a large, fluffy, natural-bristle brush. To avoid streaks, first tap the brush or blow off excess powder. Add color with gentle back-and-forth strokes; then blend to soften any edges to avoid that "war-paint" look. To achieve a subtle, contoured effect, use two blushers in the same color family: a darker, more muted shade for **defining,** and a lighter shade for **accenting**. Apply the defining shade to the hollow of the cheek and the accenting shade just above, on the "apple" of the cheek, angling upward toward the top portion of the ear. Overlap the two shades. Avoid over-contouring with blusher. Remember, blusher is color, and heavy color on the cheeks is not only outdated, but it can look streaky and unnatural. Ideally, creating angularity by contouring should be done with highlighter and contour shadow (see "Highlighter and Contour Shadow," page 35). Let nature be your best guide for placement. The sun brings color to your cheeks, forehead, temples, bridge of nose, and even the sides of your neck. Apply blusher sparingly to these areas. Blusher should always be subtle.

HINT: To achieve the look of a dewy glow to the cheeks, stroke a small amount of neutral-to-beige pearlized blusher (or frosted eye shadow) on the apple of the cheeks.

permanent makeup

One of the newest additions to the cosmetics world is permanent makeup (also called dermapigmentation, micropigmentation, or surgical skin pigmentation), which is the same as tattooing. Now you can have eyeliner, brow makeup, and lip liner twenty-four hours a day.

The process consists of implanting hypoallergenic pigment (iron oxide-based) into the second layer of the skin with a tiny needle. Mild stinging is typical, but not unbearable. The area is usually numbed with a topical anesthetic. Slight swelling occurs for a few hours. About three days later, the skin flakes off to reveal the permanent color. Permanent makeup must be performed by a qualified technician with an artistic eye to ensure proper selection of color and placement of pigment. Ideally, for safety reasons, the procedure should be done in a medical environment.

Obviously, I love the process of makeup, but I do feel that permanent makeup also serves a purpose. It could benefit a woman with poor vision, arthritis, problems with dexterity, allergies to makeup, watery eyes, or problems with contact lenses or oily skin that causes makeup to smear. Also, convenience might be a consideration for an athletic woman who wants to look good during sports or exercise. Some women simply don't like to be seen without eye makeup.

One of the most beneficial uses for permanent eye makeup is to re-create the illusion of lost lashes and brows due to hair loss induced by chemotherapy, or a condition that causes total hair loss known as alopecia areata.

Permanent makeup is also used to line and fill in the lips. It can correct irregularly shaped lips, as well as make the lips look fuller. Because of its permanence, many women find it convenient not to have to apply lip color frequently.

Permanent makeup will fade and need repeating after about four years. The average cost is between $500 and $1,000 per area.

Note: Permanent makeup is sometimes used for touching up areas of the skin that have lost pigmentation, as in the skin disorder, vitiligo (see top left photograph, page 63). Post-surgical scars, if noticeable, can also be permanently camouflaged by tattooing the lighter colored areas of the scar to match the surrounding skin.

LOSS OF HAIR

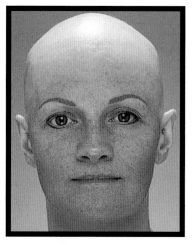

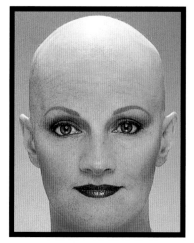

Peggy, <u>before</u> permanent makeup: Notice her lack of eyelashes and brows.

<u>After</u> permanent eyeliner and brows.

With the addition of makeup, including artificial lashes.

"I was fourteen when I started to lose my hair. It was a ten-year battle before I was totally bald. Now that I'm in my forties, I've accepted myself and don't feel any less feminine."

A natural-looking wig helps beautiful Peggy feel beautiful.

BURNS

Marni has undergone more than 100 reconstructive surgeries (and is still in the process) because of injuries resulting from a fire. Corrective makeup helps "normalize" her appearance.

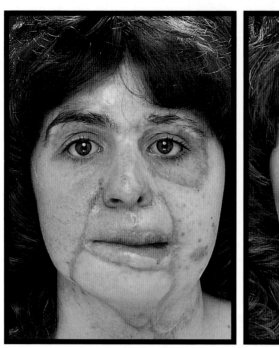

Marni (age 27), <u>before</u> makeup.

<u>After</u> makeup.

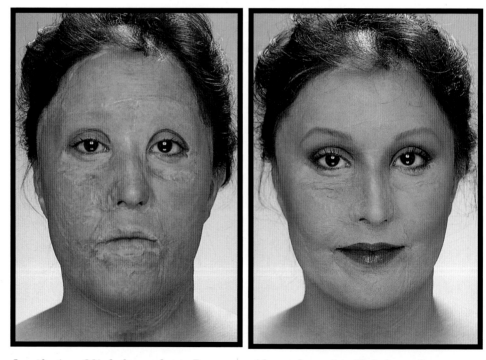

Jennifer (age 22), <u>before</u> makeup: Burn scars can easily be covered with camouflage cream.

<u>After</u> makeup: Jennifer's face takes on a more normal appearance, revealing her beautiful eyes.

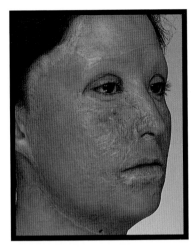

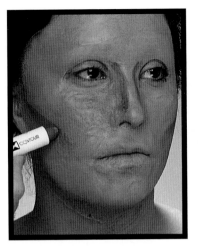

Typical of many burn survivors, Jennifer has lost her eyebrows as well as some hair. Her nose has been reconstructed, and scar tissue caused assymetry to the contour of her lips.

Use contour shadow to bring back lost shadows that camouflage cream took away. Shade sides of nose to reestablish its shape and create definition.

After eye makeup, draw on eyebrows, using a two-step process: First, create shape of brow with eye shadow applied with a firm, slant-tipped brush; then, on a diagonal, draw on hair-like strokes with pencil.

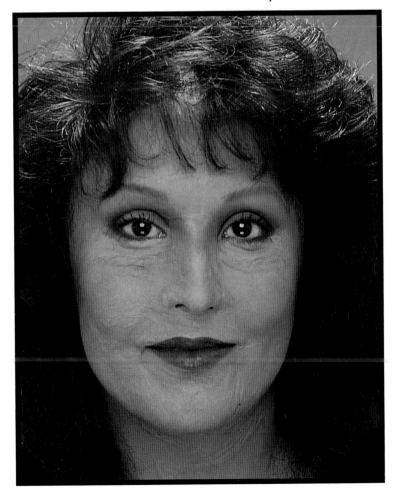

ABOVE: *Lip lining is of utmost importance for burn survivors. A normal-appearing mouth can be created by covering irregular lip line with camouflage cream, then drawing in a new natural-looking lip line before filling with color.*

RIGHT: *By bringing Jennifer's bangs forward, hair loss is concealed and focus is brought to her beautiful eyes.*

"PORT WINE STAIN" BIRTHMARK

Suepinda (age 18), <u>before</u> makeup: Port wine stain covers almost half her face.

<u>After</u> makeup.

"I never really wore makeup before, because I never knew how to properly conceal my port wine stain. People tell me I'm pretty now . . . but I still get embarrassed."

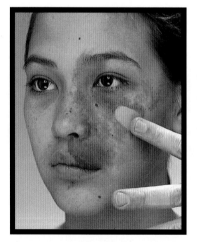

Apply camouflage cream to center of birthmark and work outward.

Use shearer coat of camouflage cream on surrounding skin. If port wine stain has affected shape of lips, as Suepinda's has, cover lips as well to be able to draw in a new lip line.

Metamorphosis is completed with color makeup following camouflage cream. Notice correction of upper lip line.

VITILIGO

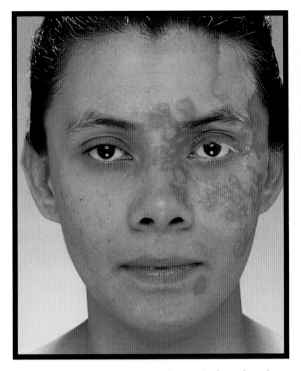

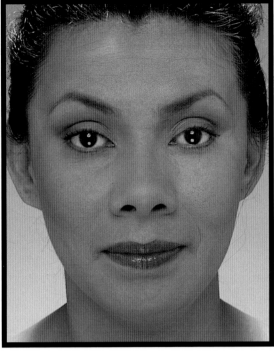

Christina (age 33), <u>before</u> makeup: Light-colored areas of vitiligo are nothing more than a lack of pigment. Even though her skin appears uneven, its texture is smooth. Because she's undergoing a repigmentation process called PUVA, white patches of skin become pink. Notice white hair in her left eyelashes.

<u>After</u> makeup: Camouflage cream covers all signs of vitiligo. White lashes are easily darkened with mascara. Tweezed brows help bring focus to her eyes.

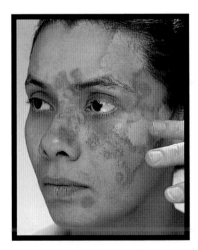

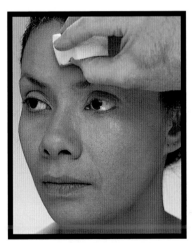

Apply camouflage cream to lighter areas first and feather into non-affected area. (Without PUVA treatment, stay within borders of white patches to avoid an odd-colored overlap—particularly for black skin or dark complexions.)

With a sponge, use a thinner coat of camouflage cream on surrounding skin.

"I was so confused when it happened. Initially no one, including doctors, knew what it was. I'm so anxious to get my color back. In the meantime, I feel great with makeup."

CLEFT LIP/PALATE

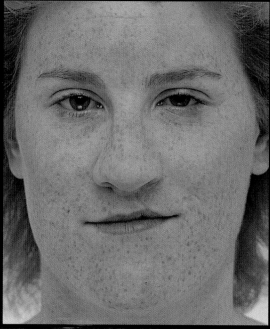

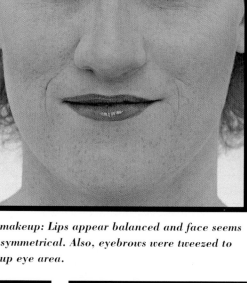

Katie (age 24), <u>before</u> makeup: Cleft lip creates a snarling appearance as well as a broad nose.

<u>After</u> makeup: Lips appear balanced and face seems more symmetrical. Also, eyebrows were tweezed to open up eye area.

"I was teased a lot in junior high school and I do everything I can to improve my looks. I went to an orthodontist which also helped correct my mouth. I've never been that good with makeup, but I'm learning. I consider myself very lucky."

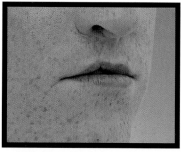

Notice thin scar above upper lip.

Hide scar by applying camouflage cream with a tiny brush; then follow with normal foundation.

Straighten tilt of mouth by raising lower side with lip liner; then fill with color.

Narrow nose by applying contour shadow along sides; then blend.

eturning to normalcy

For an individual with a facial difference, a congenital defect, or anyone whose appearance has been altered by an accident, ravaged by a disease, or changed by chemotherapy or radiation, the most expressed desire is to look normal. Those who haven't undergone this experience can't imagine the feelings of isolation and rejection that ensue.

Regardless of the degree of the problem, makeup can *always* help, and yet, specifically designed makeup techniques and product information rarely have been directed to those who could benefit most.

The wrong makeup can actually accent the disfigurement or problem. It's common for people to feel clownlike after incorrect makeup is applied and never want to use makeup again.

If you have a skin abnormality or disfigurement, don't be timid about learning to use cosmetics. First, know that you're entitled. The therapeutic value of makeup can be an important factor to help free yourself to get on with your life and take control. If you see any improvement when you look in the mirror, then it's worthwhile. Regardless of your sex, using makeup bears no more of a stigma than wearing a corrective shoe.

The main objective when using corrective cosmetics is to play down the abnormality and draw attention to other areas. There's beauty in everyone and there's always something to play up. Makeup colors should always be subdued. Avoid obvious bright colors or frosted lip colors or eye shadows, and be sure to use powder to reduce shine so that the skin becomes less reflective. Shiny surfaces draw attention to scarred, mottled, or rough skin.

CARMEN

"I came from a very old-fashioned
Italian family where vanity was
a sin. I didn't want to turn out
like a little gray-haired Italian
widow with a black shawl
over her head. Today, I'm
the artist of my face.
I'm constantly striving to
improve my canvas. But
I've learned to listen to
Mother Nature first.
Then I investigate all
the tools that God
and science offer.
Any woman who
doesn't is a fool."

Chapter 4
Looking Younger Without Cosmetic Surgery

40-Plus

"Darling, they're not making mirrors the way they used to." This wonderful quote may be humorous, but it's not as valid today as when it was originally uttered by the late actress, the outspoken Tallulah Bankhead.

Today, not only have age groups become more homogeneous, but even mothers and daughters are often difficult to distinguish from one another! Remember how old everyone looked in our parents' high school yearbook and how you thought anyone over fifty was a senior citizen? Not anymore. Blame it on the baby boomers, who have thrown out all the old rules, influenced several generations, and caused one of the great revolutions of the century—a beauty revolution! We've learned that when we label ourselves anything, we tend to become that.

So what does middle aged look like, anyway? Today, 40-plus no longer means you're over the hill. Think of Candice Bergen, Jaclyn Smith, Christie Brinkley, Cher, and Farrah Fawcett. They're all in their forties and are even more beautiful today than they were twenty years ago.

There's a direct correlation between beauty and good health, and without a doubt, youthfulness is linked to both. Thank you, Jane Fonda, Ann-Margret, Catherine Deneuve, Linda Evans, Tina Turner, Barbra Streisand, Raquel Welch, and dozens of other eternally young women in their "fabulous fifties." Gorgeous "Dallas" star Linda Gray, now a grandmother in her fifties, told me that she's never felt better about her appearance than she does now.

If the word *sexagenarian* sounds like a dirty word to you, change your outlook. Hats off to stunning Elizabeth Taylor, whose youthful attitude is paralleled by her sensational appearance, sixty-something, vibrant, and ageless Debbie Reynolds, and still stunning in her seventies Lena Horne. At sixty, silver-haired super-model Carmen's classic beauty is as striking today as it was forty years ago.

Carmen's beautiful skin is maintained by a structured routine based on a combination of information she's acquired throughout the years. She credits much of her results to dermatological procedures and smart makeup. With a Retin-A regimen (see "Retin-A: Miracle in a Jar?", page 71), she religiously stays out of the sun, wears a sun block daily, and uses a mild skin scrub twice weekly. She advocates electrolysis, having eyelashes dyed, and corrective makeup procedures. "I have very thin lips," she states. "If I don't extend over my lip line, I'd have no lips at all." By the way, Carmen does her own makeup and hair for most of her photo sessions.

Carmen believes beauty is a question of how you feel. "People always say what they *don't* like about themselves. First, say what you *do* like, then work on the rest. Do your homework, then evaluate, make choices, and be diligent."

Beauty depends on your attitude, spirit, and openness to change. Celebrate your sophistication, but don't ever lose your childlike inner self.

*M*akeup and the mature woman

Rejuvenating the face with cosmetic surgery can work wonders, but surgery may not be practical, affordable, or something you feel comfortable about doing. Corrective makeup, on the other hand, can give you an instant face-lift. Yet, rarely is the subject of makeup addressed to the mature woman. Ironically, no age group can experience the advantage of corrective makeup more than the woman over forty, particularly without the help of cosmetic surgery.

Once you learn to adapt some of these corrective steps into your makeup routine, it should become second nature to you. In fact, if a full beauty makeup takes you longer than twenty minutes, it's taking too long.

INSTANT FACE-LIFT

Being stuck in an old beauty rut is a common makeup trap. What worked in high school can date you as well as age you. This doesn't mean you have to throw out your makeup and start all over again or give up sensible cosmetic techniques that work for you. But using the wrong makeup can exaggerate lines and wrinkles. By updating your makeup to a more contemporary look and incorporating the right kind of corrective cosmetics into your daily routine, you can instantly take five to ten years off your face.

Does getting older mean wearing less makeup? Yes and no. Generally, as you age, makeup application should be more subtle, but don't confuse the no-makeup look with a washed-out or plain look. With a little practice and some makeup savvy, you can learn to create the perfect look for your face.

By the way, studies have shown that men prefer women who wear some makeup over those who wear none at all, and most men only recognize the most blatant makeup. Interestingly, another study showed that 92 percent of men over age forty-five actually preferred the over-forty-five woman who wore heavier makeup to those who wore light makeup.

Aging can wash out features that once were vibrant. Now, more than ever, color and definition are needed for emphasis. Makeup for over-forty eyes should be sophisticated, but not overdone. Avoid pastel shades. Clearer (brighter) shades of blusher and lip colors can take years off your face.

Let moderation and good judgment rule. Someone who tries to look too young with obvious makeup (or too much cosmetic surgery) looks ridiculous. For the woman over forty, makeup used incorrectly can add years to a face. What not to do may be more critical than what to do.

A Dozen "Don'ts"

1. Don't use heavy or mismatched foundation.
2. Don't apply foundation unevenly.
3. Don't apply blusher too high or too low.
4. Don't use too little, obvious, or brown-based blusher.
5. Don't use overly light under-eye concealer.
6. Don't use frosted or bright eye shadow (particularly blue).
7. Don't allow eyeliner to be hard-edged or smeary.
8. Don't overdo the mascara or use obvious false lashes.
9. Don't pencil in hard-edged or shiny, artificial-looking brows.
10. Don't use too pale, too dark, or too bright lip color.
11. Don't outline lips with dark or obvious pencil, or allow lip color to feather.
12. Don't over- or under-exaggerate lip shape.

TAKING TEN YEARS OFF YOUR FACE WITH MAKEUP

Actress Gloria DeHaven, still stunning at sixty-seven, is a wonderful example of someone who not only takes good care of her skin, but understands the value of corrective makeup. A former redhead, Gloria has let her hair become salt-and-pepper, which, she says, "I'm very satisfied with. God did a wonderful job."

Because Gloria has never had cosmetic surgery (but says she feels ready for it now), she's an ideal model to show how corrective makeup can take ten years off a face. Because everyone's face is different, you may need additional steps or you may need fewer. Corrective makeup steps are always subtle, but the cumulative result can be sensational. Whether you're forty or eighty, the principles work and can help de-age almost anyone!

GLORIA DeHAVEN

Gloria's fine features seem rather undefined before makeup.

Corrective makeup steps bring back a youthful appearance.

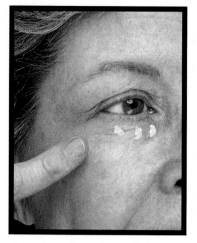

Dot concealer only on dark areas of under-eye circle (for puffiness or bags, apply a lighter shade to crease below bag, not directly on raised area).

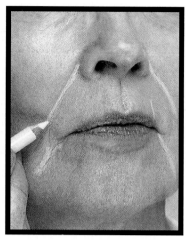

Lighten lines, wrinkles, and depressions with a thin application of light-colored concealer or concealing pencil.

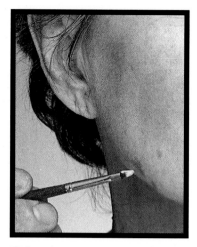

Hide age spots or other pigmented areas prior to foundation by "spot-covering" with camouflage cream.

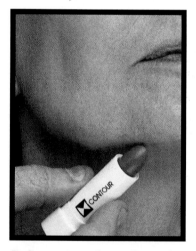

Define an irregular jawline and reduce jowls with a contour shadow.

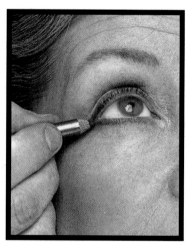

Before lining eyes, use an eye base to hold color if lids are crepey. Apply normal foundation to entire face and with a cotton swab or applicator, apply a small amount of foundation over lids to cover any discoloration; blend into tiny crevices. Lightly powder face to diminish shine and facial lines but still retain a dewy radiance (to avoid "cakiness," use minimal powder around eye area). Dust on a clear shade of blusher for color. Line eyes with a muted shade (not black), and smudge to avoid a hard line (avoid lining lower lid if you have under-eye bags or very dark circles).

Define eyes with muted tones to hide lines, wrinkles, and puffiness (for hooded eyes, be sure to darken entire hood; for very wrinkled or dry skin, use cream eye shadows or eye shadow pencils).

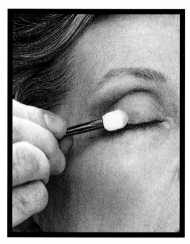

Accent eyes with light, muted colors (avoid iridescents, and be careful with brown eye shadows—they tend to age a face and create a tired appearance). Gray, blue-gray, and mauve eye shadow work well with silver hair.

Avoid obvious white highlighter under brow. Subtly accent brow bone with same (or slightly lighter) shade used on lid.

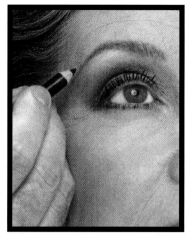

Before eyeliner and mascara, curl lashes for a wide-eyed look; then, apply mascara (lightly to lower lashes). Shape brows to form a graceful arch and fill with neu-tral-color pencil or shadow. If brows are short, extend them to elongate eye.

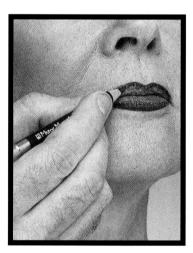

Before lip color, condition lips with a lip primer to prevent feathering; then line outside natural lip line to make lips appear fuller. Bring out mouth with clear, obvious color, but be sure to avoid an overly glossy, bright, or dark lip color. Keep a balance between lips and eyes.

Non-surgical skin fixes

As the face ages, the effects of the **Sun** become apparent, fine lines begin to form, the skin begins to lose its elasticity, and possible changes in pigmentation can occur (see "How the Face Ages," page 75). Scientific breakthroughs such as Retin-A (or its milder moisturizing formula called Renova), alpha hydroxy acids, and other non-surgical youth potions can offer solutions to common beauty problems and help combat aging.

RETIN-A: MIRACLE IN A JAR?

Retin-A, used as a means of age intervention can help reverse and retard the effects of chronic sun exposure. Although effective, it won't produce the dramatic results of a chemical peel or dermabrasion (see "Chemical Peel," page 101, and "Dermabrasion," page 104).

An acid derivative of vitamin A, Retin-A (tretinoin) is a topical drug that promotes growth of new collagen (after eight to twelve months' use) in the middle layer of the skin while thinning and peeling the outer layer. Originally prescribed (and approved by the Federal Drug Administration) to treat acne, Retin-A was found to erase fine lines and freckly spots at the same time.

But is this miracle drug Ponce de León's fountain of youth? I doubt it. Evidence has shown, though, that after four months' use, Retin-A improved the damaged, photo-aged skin (wrinkling around the eye area, roughness, sallowness, mottled pigmentation, freckles, and age spots) of middle-aged and elderly persons. Additional studies have shown that skin treated with Retin-A has improved circulation, resulting in a rosy "glow." It can also benefit very oily or acne-prone skin and actually shrink enlarged pores. The best news might be Retin-A's ability to cause precancerous spots to regress.

Retin-A requires a lifetime commitment, however, since the skin will revert to its previous condition within six months to a year after ceasing treatment.

Redness, dryness, flakiness, itchiness, or possible broken capillaries may occur while using Retin-A. Irritation normally subsides when it's used correctly and in the proper concentration. Expect to see your dermatologist every two to six weeks until side effects fade, with periodic visits thereafter. Also, ask your doctor if he or she advocates using Retin-A containing a bleaching agent (such as hydroquinone), which helps even out the skin tone when used together. Many doctors report favorable results with the two.

A "time-release" Retin-A is now being tested that is said to lessen its irritation. Millions of tiny "microsponges" are released gradually to lessen the drug's side effects.

Don't be fooled by other over-the-counter or mail-order products with sound-alike names. Retin-A is a serious drug, sold by prescription.

ALPHA HYDROXY ACIDS

Newer on the anti-aging scene are alpha hydroxy acids (AHAs), mild fruit acids that accelerate the formation of new and healthier skin by loosening the already dead skin cells. The best known AHA is glycolic acid, which is also used as a light chemical peel when professionally applied in stronger concentrations (see "Chemical Peel," page 101).

Even though AHAs are similar to Retin-A, they don't have the long list of side effects, and photosensitivity is less likely. Results are promised within one to three days with optimum effects visible after four weeks. AHAs are now available through dermatologists and cosmetic surgeons and can be purchased in lower concentrations over the counter.

high-tech youth creams

Like AHAs and Retin-A, another wrinkle fighter known as Nayad (the trade name for betaglucan), a patented yeast extract, is said to repair sun-damaged skin and even speed the healing of wounds. Creams containing the well-known antioxident vitamin E are reported to be an immune stimulant and creams containing vitamin B and vitamin A derivatives also show promise. Vitamin C–based formulations are said to improve the skin's strength, texture, and resilience. These, and many other products, can improve the texture and coloration of your skin— two elements that, when combined with cosmetics, can help restore a more youthful appearance.

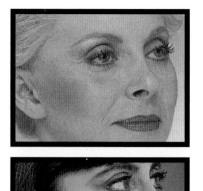

Part III

Cosmetic surgery— A Beauty Revolution

God hath given you one face
and you make yourselves another.

—SHAKESPEARE

Twenty years old.

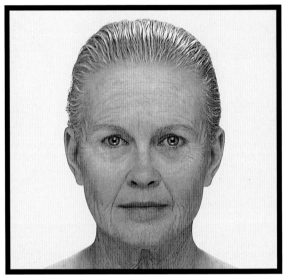

Seventy years old.

These photographs are not grandmother and granddaughter, nor are they two different people. Through the magic of computer imaging, and without any cosmetic intervention, I aged former Miss USA Courtney Gibbs Eplin by fifty years.

Chapter 5

Aging and How to Combat It

how the face ages

SLOWING DOWN THE HANDS OF TIME

Aging starts slowly, but unfortunately it accelerates as we grow older. In other words, we age more rapidly between forty-five and fifty than we do between twenty-five and thirty. We can't stop the aging process, but with the help of cosmetic treatments, as well as proper diet, exercise, and reduced stress, we have the ability to slow it down.

The "Anti-Aging Face Chart" on pages 76-77 will give you an idea of what changes may occur in your appearance from age twenty to seventy. Check the resolution column for ways to intervene if you want to fight aging at every decade.

HAVING A YOUTHFUL EDGE

Granted, aging is chronological, but it's an inexact measurement. Take a good look at your parents. If you're fortunate enough to have inherited great genes, most likely you'll age in a similar fashion (called intrinsic aging).

People who look five to ten years younger than their actual age generally maintain that advantage for life. Also, a man, particularly during his forties and fifties, can look up to ten years younger than a woman of the same age. A man's thicker skin is more resistant to sun damage and beard follicles also provide added support and elasticity.

ANTI-AGING FACE CHART

**A glimpse of what changes are likely to occur as you age—
what you can do to fight aging for every decade**

AGE	POSSIBLE FACIAL CHANGE	RESOLUTION
20s	• Skin texture and elasticity are at its prime with expression lines just beginning to form.	————
30s	• Tiny lines become visible around eyes (crow's-feet), forehead, and from nose to outside corner of mouth (nasolabial folds).	Retin-A or glycolic acid; collagen or fat injections.
	• Upper or lower eyelids accumulate fat, creating bags.	Eyelid surgery.
	• Broken capillaries occur around nose and cheeks.	Electrodesiccation (cauterization) or laser therapy.
40s	• Blotchy skin and redness occur; fine lines appear above upper lip (more common for women).	Light chemical peel.
	• Skin on neck slightly sags, with fat accumulating under chin and jowl area.	Neck contouring (liposuction).
	• Brows and eyelids droop; forehead furrows show.	Forehead-lift.
	• Upper or lower eyelids become puffy or baggy.	Eyelid surgery (particularly if not corrected in the 30s).
	• Frown lines appear; overall lines deepen.	Retin-A or glycolic acid; collagen or fat injections.
50s	• Nose appears fleshy at tip and slightly drops downward.	Nose reshaping.
	• Loss of underlying fat; neck cords appear; facial contours change due to fat and muscle redistribution.	Face-lift with fat transplantation, or cheekbone or mid-face implants.
	• Lines at outer corner of mouth ("marionette lines") appear; overall lines deepen.	Retin-A or glycolic acid; collagen or fat injections.
	• Additional broken capillaries occur; freckling.	Electrodesiccation or laser therapy; cryosurgery (freezing).
	• Lips become thinner and pale; mouth droops downward.	Lip pencil to line outside natural lip line.
	• Facial hair increases.	Bleaching, waxing, depilatories, or electrolysis.

Age	Possible Facial Change	Resolution
60s	• Bone structure changes due to actual bone shrinkage, creating reduction in chin/jaw size; cheeks hollow; jowls appear; eyelids become hooded; skin sags, loosens, wrinkles, and crinkles more.	Face-lift with eyelid surgery (first or second one); deep chemical peel or dermabrasion (full face or partial).
	• Earlobes crease, droop, and become larger.	Earlobe reduction (usually done at time of face-lift).
	• Lines deepen.	Retin-A or glycolic acid; collagen or fat injections.
	• Skin becomes thinner, creating changes in pigmentation, i.e., age spots (liver spots) and redness.	Bleaching creams to lighten; corrective makeup, like camouflage cream to spot-cover, and neutralizers to negate redness.
	• Brows and lashes become sparser.	Brow pencil and eyeliner; permanent makeup.
70s plus	• All changes continue with further acceleration.	Consider all previous options.

Bone structure is another factor that contributes to aging. Normally, strong jawlines and chins, prominent brows, and high cheekbones provide extra skeletal support so the skin remains more intact.

The skin's oil content influences aging. Oily-skinned people are known to age better than those with dry skin. People of color also tend to age well because their skin contains a higher level of melanin (pigment), which protects them from burning. Dark-haired people, as well as those with darker eyes, are also "good agers."

Aging is also caused by environmental or life-style factors (called extrinsic aging), such as exposure to the Sun.

SUN SENSE

Sun damage is the *number-one* cause of premature skin aging and occurs regardless of skin color. Did you know that the Sun is estimated to be responsible for up to 90 percent of all premature skin aging and that 80 percent of your lifetime sun damage has already occurred before the age of twenty?

We don't realize how much we're exposed to the Sun during our daily activities, especially now with our depleting ozone layer. Innocent activities, such as walking, driving, or even sitting in a sun-drenched room (where the year-round, deeper-penetrating UVA rays may reach the skin) can threaten our skin's appearance and cause wrinkling, age spots, enlarged pores, yellowish skin, loss of elasticity of the outer layer of skin, rough spots (pre-cancers), and skin cancer. Currently, one out of six Americans will develop cancer in his or her lifetime. An expected 26 percent increase of skin cancer is expected by the year 2000.

The two predominant rays (UVA and UVB) emitted from the Sun both cause sun damage. Although the UVB ray is the burning ray, the deeper penetrating UVA ray—the supposedly "safe" ray (the predominant ray of tanning booths)—is the aging ray. Some tanning booths give out five times more UVA energy than the Sun in a given period of time. Studies have also proved that skin cancer is more common in people who use lamps plus sun rather than sun alone.

Simply having a tan will not protect your skin from sun damage. A healthy-looking tan (a contradiction in terms), whether from the Sun or a tanning booth, is remembered by your skin's built-in "age memory." So, today's tan could become tomorrow's network of fine lines and discoloration.

It's never too late to begin practicing "safe sun." Use an SPF-15 sunscreen diligently—even under makeup—to guard against both rays. "Broad-spectrum" sunscreens (those with both UVA and UVB sunscreens) offer even more protection and can be purchased at most drugstores. New creams containing synthetic melanin (a colorless pigment produced by the body that turns brown on exposure to UV lights), are in development and offers sun protection without the risk of sunscreen-associated allergies.

Take advantage of the new self-tanning lotions, which offer a natural-looking tan without UV damage. You'll get the most even and natural-looking tan if you use a mild scrub before the self-tanning lotion to prep the skin first. Cover all exposed skin and avoid the brows. If you opt for a bronzing powder, apply a neutral, translucent face powder first.

INVISIBLE AGING

It has been said that *free radicals* are the "bottom line of aging." Free radicals are unstable molecules in the body that attack protein fibers such as collagen, elastin, and DNA (our genetic code). Although sun produces free radicals, so do many other factors. Although smoking doesn't seem to cause pigment changes in the skin, studies have shown that the skin of smokers ages more rapidly and tends to heal slower than that of nonsmokers. One study found that those who had smoked two packs of cigarettes a day for twenty-five years were five times more likely to get wrinkles than the nonsmokers!

Stress is another enemy. Worry, guilt, anger, and fear—all emotions that contribute to stress—show up on your face. I've seen wrinkles disappear and faces become instantly younger when stress was eliminated from someone's life.

Other contributing factors responsible for triggering premature wrinkles are improper diet, not enough water (to keep skin hydrated), weight swings, sleep deficiency, how you sleep (sleeping on your stomach in one position can cause your face to wrinkle), repeated facial expressions, lack of exercise, environmental elements, pollution, alcohol, drugs, caffeine, diuretics, and even jet travel.

'THE FIRST LADY OF COSMETIC SURGERY'

Although few admit it, *most* celebrities and an estimated 50 percent of television newscasters have had something done. No one has been more public about her quest for beauty than the "First Lady of Cosmetic Surgery," the irrepressible comic Phyllis Diller. And because of her candor, she's an inspiration to others.

Why is it that Phyllis looks so much better now than she did at age forty? "If you want to age gracefully," she says, "then take up ballet! I knew I had to make some changes. It's not easy to remember the exact moment I decided to have a face-lift. It might have been when I was twelve years old and woke up every morning and said, 'Mirror, mirror on the wall . . . I don't want to hear it.' You've heard the expression 'face value'? I was in debt!"

While she teases "no two parts of my body are the same age," Phyllis takes looking good very

Phyllis at forty.

PHYLLIS' PROCEDURES

1970: Teeth straightened
1971: Face-lift; nose reshaping; eyelid surgery
(upper and lower lids)
1980: Teeth bonded (see right photograph, page 80)
1981: "Mini" face-lift
1985: Forehead-lift; nose reshaping
(revision); eyelid surgery (lower lids again);
cheek augmentation; permanent eyeliner
1986: Chemical peel
1987: Fat injections (lines from nose to mouth)

Phyllis at seventy-five.

"We're all created equal . . . Bull! We're not. Some people look like Grace Kelly and some people look like me. I've worked so hard on staying young, it's beginning to age me. I have deep-set eyes with eyebrows that used to grow so low, I looked like an unemployed librarian! I needed my eyes opened up, so I shaved them off every day and drew in new ones . . . badly! Also, my nose was so long that it affected the proper balance between the upper, middle, and lower third of my face. My skin was freckled and lined and my front teeth were crooked, which always created a shadow. My old face got me where I am—it was a fine face but it wasn't pretty to live with."

seriously. She's not only de-aged her face with cosmetic surgery, but she's refined her features as well. Phyllis heals quickly, is in excellent health, and has a positive attitude. This makes her a perfect candidate for cosmetic surgery.

Take a look at Phyllis before makeup, then study her improvements after makeup. She's a terrific example of what corrective makeup can accomplish and how it further enhances the results of cosmetic surgery.

Phyllis Diller (today) <u>before</u> makeup: With cosmetic surgery, Phyllis's features are well balanced but still undefined without makeup. Her nose has been reshaped, cheekbones made a little higher, bags removed from under eyes, skin texture smoothed as well as "de-freckled," and her teeth have been redone.

Phyllis Diller (today) <u>after</u> makeup: Makeup not only enhances improvements of prior surgeries but makes Phyllis look even younger. Her eyes appear bigger, brighter, and more uplifted by creating a three-dimensional look with eye makeup, adding artificial lashes, and completely drawing in natural-looking brows (see photographs, page 52). A soft peach blusher brings color to her skin, and her lips appear fuller by lining outside her natural lip line. A muted orange-red lip color makes her new "pearly-whites" seem even whiter. Not bad for seventy-five!

Chapter 6
Is Facial Surgery for You?

realistic expectations

Cosmetic surgery may make you look younger, improve your looks, and even boost your self-confidence, but it's not a cure-all for all your problems. It's not going to save a failing marriage or guarantee finding a mate.

People with low self-esteem and feelings of inadequacy, or persons with an imagined ugliness condition called body dismorphic disorder (BDD), who become addicted to cosmetic surgery (cosmetic surgery "junkies") have set unrealistic goals for themselves in their search for perfection. By changing an ideal that they'll never achieve. They repeatedly try to change their looks and are rarely satisfied. Cosmetic surgery should never be desired as an end to a means. With realistic goals, the benefits outweigh the risks.

finding a cosmetic surgeon

Years ago, movie stars and wealthy matrons flew to Paris or Brazil for cosmetic surgery. Today, although California, New York, Florida, and Texas are considered the meccas of cosmetic surgery, brilliant surgeons practice their craft in almost every major city in the United States. Revolutionary techniques are no longer kept secret, and endless information is shared among surgeons worldwide through educational seminars, global symposiums and conferences, and closed-circuit television (through which operations are simultaneously performed and transmitted via satellite).

Selecting the right surgeon is critical. In fact, it's a good idea to see two or three doctors

FACIAL SURGERY AT A GLANCE

An introduction to the most commonly performed cosmetic procedures

PROCEDURE	TIME	DISCOMFORT	RECOVERY TIME	LIFE OF OPERATION	POSSIBLE COMPLICATIONS	COST
Eyelid Surgery "Blepharoplasty" Bags, folds, excess skin and fat are removed.	1 to 2 hours	Minor soreness; light swelling and watery eyes; possible sensitivity to light.	3 to 10 days (scars fade in 9 to 12 weeks)	Lower lid fairly permanent; 7 to 15 years for upper	Difficulty closing eyes (usually temporary); lower lid may pull away from eye (rare); tearing problem (rare and usually temporary); loss of vision (extremely rare).	$2,500 to $5,000
Nose Reshaping "Rhinoplasty" Length and shape of nose are remodeled to conform to facial proportions.	30 minutes to 2 hours	Virtually no pain; headaches can occur if surgical packing is used; short-term difficulty in breathing.	1 week (majority of swelling is down in 3 months and remainder of swelling could take 6 to 12 months)	Permanent	Numbness, infection (rare); contour irregularities; difficulty breathing; diminished sense of smell; formation of scar tissue.	$2,000 to $6,000
Face-lift "Rhytidectomy" Skin and facial muscles are tightened and excess skin is removed.	2 to 4 hours	Minor discomfort, tightness, numbness.	1½ to 3 weeks (incision scars often feel lumpy at 6 weeks but flatten by 12 weeks; redness fades by 6 months)	5 to 10 years	Numbness on face and neck; loss of hair at suture line; skin pulled too tight; lumpiness (temporary); bleeding under the skin (rare); nerve damage (rare); partial facial paralysis (rare); dry skin (temporary).	$2,500 to $10,000
Forehead-lift "Coronoplasty" Removes excess skin to lift sagging eyebrows and diminish frown lines and horizontal wrinkles.	1 to 2 hours	Some pain and tenderness which diminishes after 3 or 4 weeks.	1 to 2 weeks	5 to 10 years	Numbness in top of scalp (usually temporary); hair thinning (temporary); bleeding under skin ("hematoma"—rare); nerve damage (rare); itching (temporary).	$1,500 to $5,000
Neck Contouring "Submental Lipectomy" (Liposuction) Fat deposits are removed to reduce double chin.	30 minutes to 1 hour	Some swelling; tenderness.	1 week	Usually permanent (puffiness for 2 weeks; stiffness up to 6 weeks)	Contour irregularities; lumpiness (usually temporary); numbness (temporary).	$800 to $2,500

Procedure	Time	Discomfort	Recovery	Duration of Results	Risks	Cost
Fat Injections Fat is extracted from body, then used to fill wrinkles, furrows, and depressions.	30 minutes to 1 hour	Some pain from local anesthetic.	3 to 4 days (minor bruising and swelling)	3 to 18 months (with possible permanent correction)	Redness; itching; swelling; lumpiness; infection (rare).	$500 to $2,000 per procedure
Collagen Injections Wrinkles, furrows, and depressions are raised and smoothed.	2 to 10 minutes each injection	Some pain during injection.	2 to 3 hours (possible small bruises for a few days)	3 to 18 months	Allergic reactions; redness; itching; swelling; lumpiness.	$200 to $400 per injection
Chemical Peel "Chemabrasion" Outer layer of skin is chemically "burned" to remove age lines, superficial scars, and irregular pigmentation.	1 to 2 hours (full face)	Some pain and burning for about 2 to 4 days; some blistering and swelling; itchiness.	2 to 3 weeks (scabbing or crusting for first week; redness fades in 6 weeks with gradual fading over a 4-month period)	5 to 10 years for deep peel; 6 months to 3 years for light peel	Infection and inflammation (rare); irregular skin pigmentation (usually lighter); scarring; white heads ("milea"); enlarged pores.	$2,000 to $4,500
Dermabrasion Fine lines and acne scars are smoothed by gently "sanding" with a rotary wire brush.	30 minutes to 1 hour (full face)	Some pain and burning for about 2 to 4 days; some blistering and swelling; itchiness.	2 to 3 weeks (scabbing or crusting for first week; redness fades in 6 weeks with gradual fading over a 4-month period)	5 to 10 years for wrinkles; permanent for acne scars	Infection and inflammation (rare); irregular skin pigmentation; scarring; white heads ("milea"); enlarged pores.	$1,000 to $3,500
Chin Augmentation "Mentoplasty" Enlargement of a small or recessed chin with an implant.	30 minutes to 1 hour	Some swelling, pain, and achiness during first 2 days.	1 to 2 weeks	Permanent, but reversible	Infection (rare); nerve damage (rare); implant could shift or be rejected.	$1,000 to $2,500
Cheek Augmentation "Malarplasty" Enhancement for enlargement of cheekbones with implants.	45 minutes to 1 hour	Stiffness and swelling.	1 week	Permanent, but reversible	Difficulty speaking from numbness (temporary); infection (rare); implant could shift or be rejected.	$1,500 to $2,500
Ear Correction "Otoplasty" Cartilage of protruding ears is reshaped and pinned back.	1½ to 2 hours	Some soreness; throbbing the first day.	1 week	Permanent	Contour irregularities; numbness (rare); infection (rare).	$1,500 to $4,500

Prices will vary depending on geographical location, type of facility, and extent of surgery.
This information was provided by The American Society of Plastic and Reconstructive Surgeons, The American Academy of Facial Plastic and Reconstructive Surgery, and The American Academy of Cosmetic Surgery, as well as by physicians and patients.

before making any decision, and always check his or her credentials before scheduling a consultation. Recommendations from friends who have had successful surgery is a good way to begin. Your family doctor can also refer you to a reputable cosmetic surgeon. A surgeon's hospital affiliation is another factor worth considering. For a doctor to be granted surgical privileges in a hospital, he or she must have demonstrated competency. Shop for expertise and experience. Never shop for a bargain.

Be leery of surgeons who seem to be advertising in every place possible or lunch-hour procedures or other "quick fixes." Any licensed physician who wants to practice cosmetic surgery can call himself or herself a plastic or cosmetic surgeon. Any doctor can legally claim to be "board-certified," without mentioning that the certification is in something other than plastic surgery. Be sure to choose a physician who is certified by one of the twenty-three specialty boards recognized by the American Board of Medical Specialties. For plastic surgeons, the American Board of Plastic Surgery is recognized by the American Board of Medical Specialties.

Another indication of a qualified surgeon is membership in the American College of Surgeons, which is an additional honor to all board-certified surgeons. This extra certification procedure allows a doctor to affix the letters FACS (Fellow of the American College of Surgeons) to his or her name, following M.D. Keep in mind, however, that a doctor who is board certified may not necessarily be first-rate.

If you happen to select someone other than a board-certified plastic surgeon, be sure the physician's specialty or area of expertise relates directly to the cosmetic procedure that you want to have done. You can find out what specialty a doctor is certified in by going to your local library and looking up his or her name in *The Directory of Medical Specialists* and *The Compendium of Certified Medical Specialists* (see "Resources," page 121 for names and addresses of medical organizations).

the consultation

Your consultation is one of the most important times you'll spend during your beauty quest. Doctors actually appreciate a better-informed patient. Be prepared for your consultation. Make a list of questions ahead of time and don't be afraid to ask anything, no matter how trivial you might think the question is. If you don't understand an answer, ask the doctor to be more explicit. He or she should answer without hesitation. Be specific. Also, ask for a copy of his or her curriculum vitae (commonly called a CV), which lists a doctor's professional qualifications. Find out how many procedures pertaining to your particular surgery he or she has performed and ask about how you'll look just after surgery.

Be sure the doctor has a caring attitude and gives you adequate time to discuss your needs. Look at the doctor's "before and after" photographs, but keep in mind that these are likely to be the best of his or her examples.

Some doctors take time to make sketches or work with photographs, so it's not a bad idea to bring pictures of yourself as well as photos of others to discuss what results you desire. These can help the surgeon get an indication of what you have in mind as well as determine if your goal is realistic.

Many surgeons use computer imaging to show the anticipated surgical result. These computers are an excellent means of communication for both you and your doctor. But there is a drawback. Since these images are still only a prediction, a patient must be made aware that he or she is viewing only an indication of the possibilities. Video is a digitized image, surgery is never exacting, and healing is inconsistent from patient to patient.

I usually tell my female clients to wear some makeup for their consultation so that the doctor can see how they usually look. (Avoid foundation though when consulting for peels.)

Some doctors are known to take longer than

others in surgery. How fast or slow a surgeon works is not an indication of excellence or expertise. The results of his or her work should be the only determining factor.

Consultations usually range from $50 to $100 and in some cases the fee is applied toward the surgery.

the decision is yours

The decision to have cosmetic surgery is very personal and is something you do for yourself and no one else. Asking family and friends for advice about whether or not to have cosmetic surgery is not always a good idea, because it's difficult for those close to you to be objective since they love you the way you are.

It's very important to have someone you trust be with you after surgery. Ideally, the person you choose to take care of you during your recovery should be supportive of your surgery.

what to expect

Some post-surgical side effects can appear worse than they actually are. By being informed ahead of time, you'll know that the changes in your appearance are the normal, temporary aftereffects of surgery and that they'll disappear. In the meantime, the corrective makeup you learned about can help you face the world looking your best for an "unselfconscious recovery."

There are three temporary aftereffects of surgery that can be disguised with cosmetics: *incision lines, discoloration,* and *swelling.* Generally, if your procedure required incisions, you can usually apply cosmetics to cover incision lines twenty-four hours after stitches have been removed, as long as incisions are completely closed. Always check with your doctor first. Following most procedures, you should avoid exfoliants, tightening masks, abrasive pads, and skin-care products containing alcohol and acetone. Resume your former makeup and skin-care routine approximately six weeks after surgery.

As with most surgery, there's always some trade-off. There's no such thing as an "invisible" scar since a scar is a direct result of a cut and part of the healing process. Generally, people with thick, oily skin may not heal as well as fair-skinned individuals. Some people tend to form raised scars called hypertrophic scars (sometimes referred to as keloids). Darker-skinned people, such as Asians and blacks, are more likely to have this problem, although fair-skinned individuals can form hypertrophic scars as well. Remember that conscientious surgeons strive for inconspicuous scars (see "Scar Correction," page 109).

People with positive attitudes typically heal faster. Surgery is serious, but remember, you're not sick.

Although most people are satisfied with their surgeries, results are not always predictable. Redos are not uncommon. In fact, one in ten surgeries needs some fixing. Cosmetic surgery, however, carries the same 2-percent rate of serious complications as most surgical procedures.

the new you

People typically respond to aesthetic surgery by commenting on how rested, younger, or better the person appears. It's your decision whether or not to share your experience with others.

Many people are disappointed when their surgery goes unnoticed because they think the results aren't good enough. This is actually a compliment to your surgeon since your goal is to look better, not different.

If you do prefer to keep your surgery private, deliberately changing your hairstyle or hair color, redoing your makeup, or switching to contact lenses after surgery is a good idea. People will think the new you is a result of those changes.

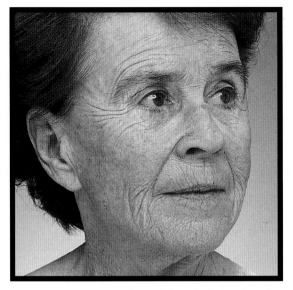

Ginny (age 65), <u>before</u> face-lift and chemical peel.

Four months <u>after</u> face-lift, and one month after chemical peel: Makeup enhances and maximizes the amazing results of Ginny's surgery. Notice how tweezing and reshaping the brows make her eyes appear even younger.

"I had my eyes done thirteen years ago before my face started to wrinkle. I think smoking combined with years in the sun playing tennis probably aged my face even more. Because of my wrinkles, I never felt comfortable wearing makeup prior to my surgery. But I never felt like the 'senior' I became. I had a very easy recovery period. I didn't even need a pain pill. Now I see a new person."

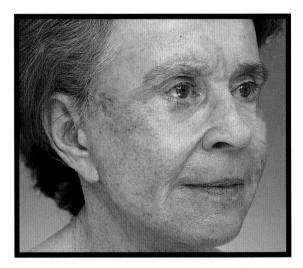

Redness on Ginny's face is temporary and due to a chemical peel. This is Ginny the same day as the photo with makeup!

Chapter 7

Rejuvenating Your Face and Balancing Your Features with Cosmetic Surgery

rebuilding and resurfacing

Rejuvenating the face can be compared to refurbishing a worn sofa. The frame must be repaired before it's covered with new fabric. In cosmetic surgery, there are two basic ways to de-age the face: **rebuilding**—repairing the facial framework (i.e., eyelid surgery, face-lift, forehead-lift, neck contouring, and facial implants and fillers); and **resurfacing**—improving the texture of the skin (i.e., chemical peels and dermabrasion).

Multiple procedures done simultaneously ("twofers") are quite common. A face-lift (including neck-lift) combined with eyelid surgery and/or a forehead-lift is the most typical. The benefits include lower cost, convenience, and less risk since the patient isn't subjected to surgery and anesthesia again. This doesn't mean you should ask the doctor for a face-lift just because you're having your eyes done. Cosmetic surgery isn't preventive.

Some doctors feel that multiple procedures have the advantage of creating superior results. Manipulating one area of the face, they say, can influence the look of another area and create better results. It's up to you to weigh all considerations.

The photographs and informantion ahead explore the most popular procedures available today. Refer to the "Facial Surgery at a Glance" chart on pages 82-83 for more information.

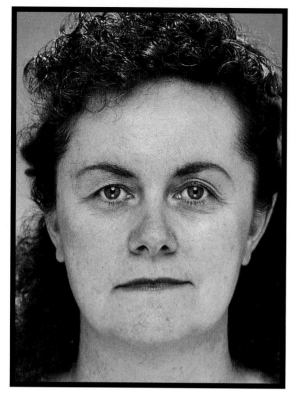

Stephanie (age 47), <u>before</u> eyelid surgery (her makeup).

Three weeks <u>after</u> surgery (my makeup): Old eye makeup must be adjusted after surgery. Also, notice Stephanie's improved jawline, which was achieved with a face-lift performed simultaneously.

<u>Before</u> surgery: Stephanie's upper lids are prematurely sagging, and her left lid is even lower than her right.

Three weeks <u>after</u> surgery: Lids now appear symmetrical; eyes are less puffy and seem larger.

Three weeks <u>after</u> surgery: A thin, pink incision line appears on upper lids.

eyelid surgery (blepharoplasty)

Because the skin around the eyes is the thinnest skin of the body, it's one of the first areas to age (see "How the Face Ages," page 75). Genetics also plays a big role. It's not uncommon, in fact, for people in their early twenties to benefit from eyelid surgery (see top photographs, page 92).

Eyelid surgery is one of the most popular and least invasive of all procedures. It refreshes a sad and tired looking face by removing extra skin, bags, and pouches from under and over the eyes. This rejuvenates the eye without changing its shape. Eyelid surgery doesn't correct droopy brows (see "Forehead-Lift," page 97) or eliminate crow's-feet (see "Chemical Peel," page 101 and "Dermabrasion," page 104).

Today's eyelid surgery is very conservative, with less skin removed than in the past. Now, for women, the more hooded, almond-shaped eye with a lower brow and a less visible upper lid has become more fashionable than the once favorable large, sunken lid with a high arched brow.

the eyelid surgery procedure

To correct the upper lid, an incision is made in the natural crease of the lid. The skin is separated from the muscle and fat, excess skin and fat are removed, and the incision is closed. Bags, which are an accumulation of fat in the lower lid, are removed by either cutting the fat away or melting it with an electrically heated probe or laser. Another procedure for bag removal (called transconjuctival blepharoplasty) entails making a tiny incision *inside* the lid, leaving no visible scar. This is only possible if there's no excess skin that would require trimming.

Because the skin around the eyes is very thin, it's one of the fastest areas to heal. Stitches are normally used on both top and bottom lids and are removed about five days later. Normally upper incision lines fade to barely visible in less than two months. Lower incisions, being close to the lash line, normally disappear completely. After surgery, the eyes will be very puffy with black-and-blue discoloration around them and on the face as well. This can be hidden with camouflage cream. Makeup and contact lenses can be worn in about a week or as soon as stitches are removed. Lightly tinted glasses can be helpful to minimize the appearance of discoloration and swelling.

Removal of too much skin from the lower lid can cause problems with tearing (dry eyes), an inability to completely close the eyes, and an odd, wide-eye stare, revealing too much white-of-the-eye below the iris. Usually these complications can be surgically corrected. However, of all facial cosmetic surgery procedures, eyelid surgery is reported to have the least amount of redos.

CORRECTIVE MAKEUP AFTER EYELID SURGERY

Post-op incision lines and discoloration are very easy to cover after eyelid surgery. Concealer and camouflage cream are too thick for the thin, delicate skin of the upper lid. Instead, use a normal foundation to avoid makeup buildup that could cake or separate in the eye's crease. With a clean cotton swab, apply the foundation to the incision line and any discoloration on the upper (or lower) lid (concealer or camouflage cream can be used on the lower lid). Then, use a cotton ball to apply loose setting powder to seal the foundation. With a soft, clean brush, apply matte eye shadow directly over the incision line. Use muted shades, such as browns and grays. Line with a soft pencil or eye shadow. Mascara should be water-soluble and fiber-free.

CRISTINA FERRARE

"Sagging eyelids run in my family. I finally had to correct them when one of my eyelids began to impair my vision. I also had my lower lids corrected from inside without an incision. After the surgery, people actually thought I lost weight!"

Cristina Ferrare
at forty-two.

Apply eye shadow over incision line to disguise any telltale trace.

Apply a thin layer of foundation over healed incision line and any discoloration.

Outline lower lid to hide faint incision line.

SALLY STRUTHERS

"When I was twenty-two, my manager noticed that my upper eyelids looked puffy and sort of hung over my eyelashes a bit in my publicity photographs. She recommended I have those folds of skin removed. Three days later, I had the procedure. Three days after that, I put on makeup and no one knew. Although it didn't utterly change my eye shape in any way, I feel it gave my eyes a larger appearance. My manager gave me very good advice."

Forty-one-year-old woman __before__ eyelid surgery (upper and lower lids). Notice how loose folds in lid hide natural eye crease.

Two years __after__ surgery: The lid, crease, and brow bone are now three distinct areas. All traces of incisions have totally disappeared.

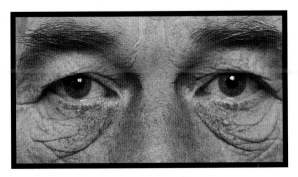

Fifty-three-year-old man __before__ eyelid surgery (upper and lower lids).

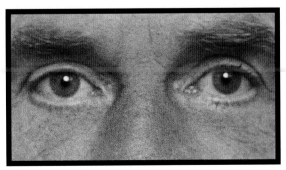

Four months __after__ surgery.

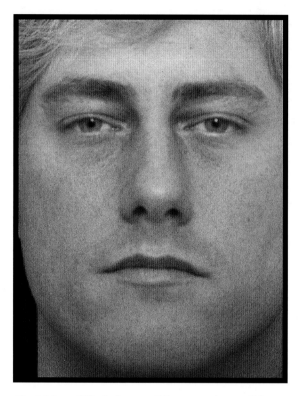

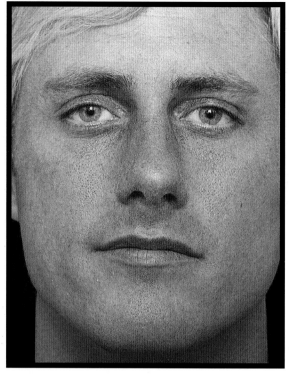

David (age 29), <u>before</u> eyelid surgery (upper lids only): David felt that premature puffiness in his upper lids made him look tired.

Four months <u>after</u> surgery: David's face appears refreshed and his eyes look larger.

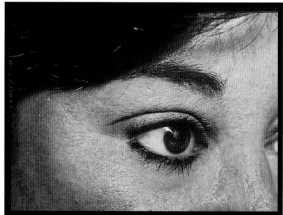

Thirty-four-year-old Asian woman <u>before</u> eyelid surgery (upper and lower lids): Drooping lids create a "hound dog" effect, which can impair vision.

Seven years <u>after</u> surgery: Lids appear evident. A forehead-lift was done simultaneously to ensure longer-term correction of eyes—this also eliminated her frown line (see "Forehead-Lift," page 97)."

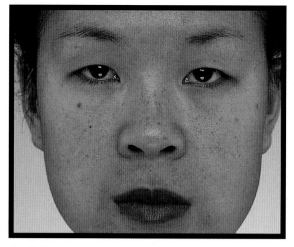

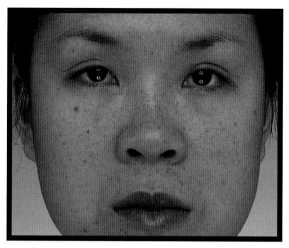

Linda (age 30), <u>before</u> eyelid surgery (upper lids only).   *Three months <u>after</u> surgery (without makeup).*

"My eyelids got so heavy, I had to constantly raise my eyebrows to keep my eyes open. My eyes started to look small and puffy. Whatever I did with my eye makeup didn't work and I became very frustrated. I wanted more of a lid, but didn't want to look Caucasian. Since the surgery, I feel more confident when I look someone in the eye. And my husband is ecstatic with the results!"

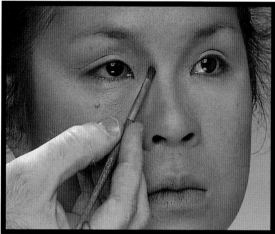

Three months <u>after</u> surgery (with makeup): Eye makeup creates more dimension and makes Linda's eyes appear even larger.   *A neutral-color eye shadow (gray-brown) originating at the beginning of brow and continuing into sides of nose adds more dimension. It reduces the fatness of Linda's face and further opens up her eyes.*

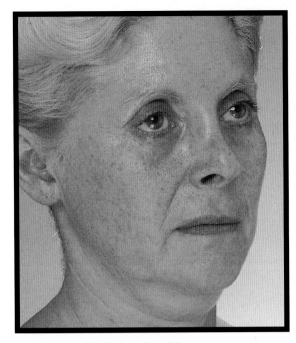

Angela (age 53), *before* face-lift.

Ten days *after* surgery (with makeup): Surgery has recaptured Angela's youth and beauty. Lower lids and nose reshaping were done simultaneously. Corrective makeup hides all temporary bruises, puffiness, redness, and incision lines during healing period (see photograph at left).

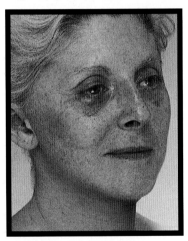

"I had my eyes done six years ago. But now that I'm older, I felt I needed to do more because I really looked tired. I also had my nose fixed when I was sixteen, but it was not a classic nose. The face-lift was a little uncomfortable, but not terrible, and it gave me that 'lift' I really needed."

ABOVE: Ten days *after* surgery (without makeup): This is the same day as the photo with makeup!

RIGHT: *Before* face-lift: Notice jowls (the number-one indication for a face-lift) and loose neck.

FAR RIGHT: Ten days *after* surgery (with makeup): Neck muscle is lifted and liposuction performed under chin. Also, indentation in bridge of nose is filled with grafting material (an implant).

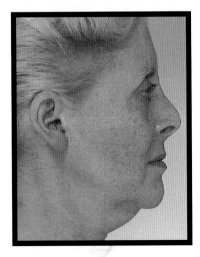

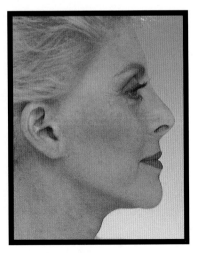

face-lift (rhytidectomy)

No longer are people waiting until they're sixty to have a face-lift. In fact, many doctors believe early face-lifts (before age fifty) last longer because the skin itself is stronger. Healing is also easier and quicker at a younger age. Some of my clients who have early face-lifts do so to maintain a more youthful appearance for a longer period. Also the results are less drastic.

THE FACE-LIFT PROCEDURE

The face-lift is the workhorse of facial rejuvenation. It helps correct sagging cheeks, jowls, an uneven jawline, and a loose' neck ("turkey wattle"). However, it won't remove fine wrinkles, because the procedure doesn't change the skin's texture (see "Chemical Peel," page 101 and "Dermabrasion," page 104).

Although face-lifts have been performed for more than seventy years, recent innovations have totally altered surgical techniques. Some people still think face-lifts give the face an artificial, mannequin look, with an overly stretched mouth, taut skin, and obvious scarring about the ears and face. When skillfully done by qualified sur-geons, however, face-lifts now appear very natur-al and last longer than they did in the past.

Today's face-lift almost always balances the face with the neck. Neck-lifts are usually done at the same time. Typically, the procedures for both involve operating on the underlying muscle and tissue beneath the skin (known as a composite or deep plane face-lift, or subperiosteal face-lift), instead of tightening only sagging skin. This rejuvenates the entire face by lifting the facial contour upward. It also can help reduce the lines from the outside corners of the nostrils to the outer corners of the mouth (called the nasolabial fold). The multi-layered procedure can some-times alter the expression somewhat, and recov-ery time is generally longer.

Incisions are made within the hairline starting at the temple, and continue downward in front of (or partially inside) the ear, then around the ear-lobe to the nape of the neck behind the ear (the hair doesn't have to be shaved). The only scar that might remain over time is a small horizontal scar behind the ear, which is normally hidden with the hair (see top left photograph, page 97). Having the incision placed within the ear shouldn't be a determining factor for choosing a surgeon. Depending upon your skin type and col-oring, surgeons often have good reason to opt for either method. Also, for men, incisions within the ear are less common because of beard growth from the sideburns.

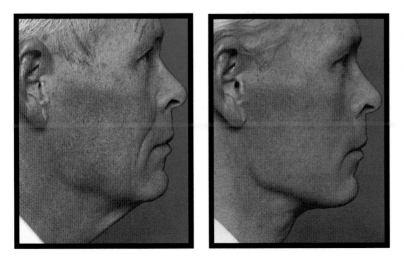

FAR LEFT: Forty-nine-year-old man _before_ face-lift.

LEFT: Two months _after_ surgery: No trace of incisions.

Because ears grow with age (particularly the earlobe), reducing large ears in conjunction with a face-lift can be beneficial (the earlobe shouldn't comprise more than 25 percent of the length of the ear). A "lobe-lift" consists of removing a pie-shaped wedge of the lobe, then bringing the edges together with a few dissolving stitches.

The "mini-lift" (tightening of the upper face), still popular with some surgeons, may be a simpler procedure than the full face-lift for less money and a shorter recovery time, but be prepared for a mini-result.

Laser face-lifts are a newer innovation. The procedure is the same, except that the surgeon uses a laser rather than a scalpel to make the incisions. Some doctors feel that lasers produce better quality scars, less bleeding, and faster recovery time. But don't be lured by the high-tech image. Because laser equipment is expensive, costs are normally built into the surgery, and laser's advantages are still questionable.

Faces generally lose elasticity after considerable weight loss. It's advisable to have a face-lift *after* weight loss, and in fact, even five pounds under your desired weight (avoid rapid weight loss within two weeks of surgery).

After a face-lift, the face remains swollen for about five days and puffy for about three weeks. Stiffness and numbness can last as long as six weeks. Bandages and stitches are usually removed after five days, but skin staples in the hair usually remain from one to two weeks. The

JULIET PROWSE

Juliet Prowse at fifty-seven.

"I've always worn a lot of theatrical makeup. My eyes were the very first thing I had done, because I couldn't continue the eye shadow in the crease of my eye. When I turned fifty, I had a little 'lift' after I noticed some jowls start to appear. Now, I'm noticing the 'cords' on my neck, and I'm thinking of having a neck-lift."

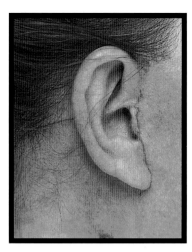

This typical face-lift incision line can be hidden with camouflage cream.

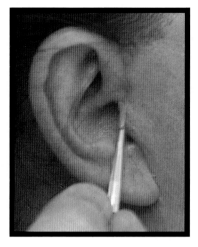

Using a clean, tiny brush, apply camouflage cream directly over healed incision line; then, with fingertip, gently feather into surrounding skin.

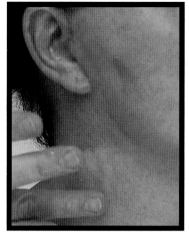

Face-lifts can produce bruising and discoloration on face and neck. Gently pat camouflage cream over these areas to hide marks during healing stage.

hair can be shampooed around three days after surgery (baby shampoos are recommended), and a cool hair dryer can be used. Wait at least two weeks for hot curlers or curling irons (and about a month for coloring or perming hair). Corrective makeup can usually be worn as soon as the stitches are removed or when approved by your doctor (avoid any scrubbing of the face for a week or two).

Women who normally wear their hair up or off their face should consider changing their hairstyle prior to a face-lift so that incision lines can be hidden in the hair during the healing phase. It's also a good idea for men to grow their sideburns longer prior to a face-lift so that the ears can be covered.

CORRECTIVE MAKEUP AFTER A FACE-LIFT

Temporary post-op incision lines and discolorations are easily covered with corrective makeup. Bruising may fade from blue to green to yellow. Incisions lines become less red over time.

forehead-lift (coronoplasty)

The face ages from the forehead down (see "How the Face Ages," page 75). One of the most visible signs of aging occurs when the eyebrows droop and the upper eyelids become hooded. The forehead-lift (also called brow-lift or coronal-lift) is one of the most effective rejuvenating procedures for creating a younger, more refreshed appearance. By raising the brows and reducing furrows in the forehead, the procedure opens up the eyes, produces a tight, smooth forehead and eliminates a scowling or angry appearance. Men's brows should never be lifted too high. This can be feminizing (see "Correcting the Brows," page 50).

Today's forehead-lift procedure has been refined to minimize the look of a perpetual surprise, which often resulted from previous methods.

Forehead-lifts are normally performed in conjunction with a face-lift and eyelid surgery to remedy drooping eyebrows due to a loss of skin tone in the forehead. It's important to distinguish droopy brows from excess eyelid tissue to avoid having excess eyelid skin unnecessarily cut away by overzealous surgeons.

THE FOREHEAD-LIFT PROCEDURE

Incisions are made across the head and behind the hairline from ear to ear. Sections of muscle are often removed from the forehead and between the eyebrows to eliminate frown lines. The skin is pulled upward, excess skin is removed, and the incision is closed.

People with receding hairlines or high foreheads may not be suitable candidates for this type of surgery. An alternative modification would be an incision along the hairline (which might leave a slight scar) or an incision actually within a forehead furrow or along the upper border of the eyebrow (called a browpexy), which is typically performed on men. Temporal lifts (with incisions hidden within the hair of the temples) can offer men some brow correction as well. Some doctors believe that new innovations, such as the laser lift, may offer favorable results. The procedure consists of a small two-inch incision at the center of the hairline instead of the surgical ear-to-ear cut. Recovery time is faster with less chance of an overly raised-eyebrow look.

After surgery, the entire head is bandaged. Temporary numbness and itching usually occur. Headaches are common for one or two days. As soon as the bandages are removed (in a day or two), the hair can be shampooed and styled with a cool dryer. Skin staples are removed within two weeks. Swelling will occur and bruising will move downward, disappearing within two weeks. Camouflage cream can be used to cover the bruising as soon as the bandages are removed or when approved by your doctor.

Thirty-three-year-old woman __before__ forehead-lift.

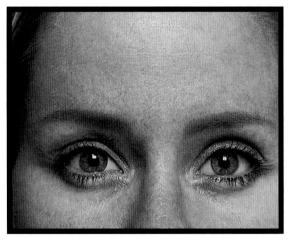

Five months __after__ surgery: A youthful eye has been created even though eyelid surgery was not performed. Notice smoother forehead, elimination of frown lines between eyes, raised brow, and an apparent eyelid.

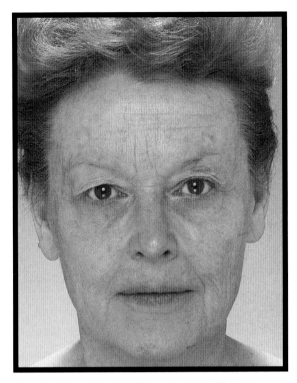

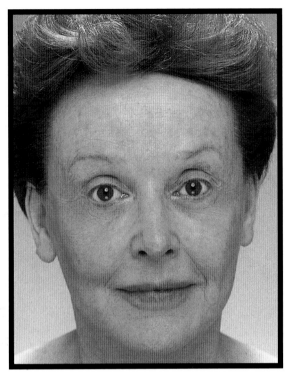

Dorothy (age 59) <u>before</u> forehead-lift, face-lift, and eyelid surgery: Face appears tired with scowling expression. Eye shadow would be difficult to use.

Three months <u>after</u> surgery (without makeup): Scowling expression is gone. Because Dorothy had excess eyelid skin, the combination of eyelid surgery and a forehead-lift produced optimum results for her eyes.

Three months <u>after</u> surgery (with makeup): Makeup helps complement results of surgery. Now Dorothy can easily apply eye makeup.

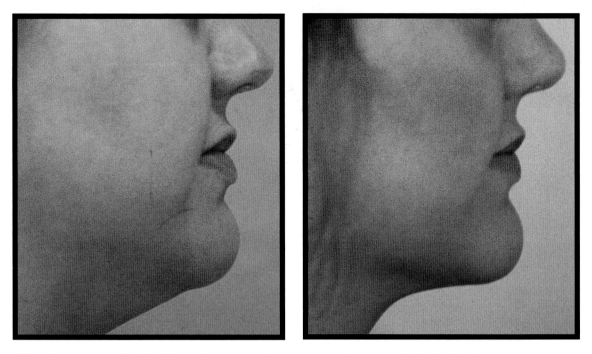

This eighteen-year-old girl's full neck is common in many normal-weight individuals. Neck contouring is accomplished by suctioning fat through a tiny incision below chin.

neck contouring (submental lipectomy)

Regardless of body weight, the neck can appear full or develop a double chin due to excess fat.

THE NECK CONTOURING PROCEDURE

Contouring the neck and face with liposuction (also called suction assisted lipectomy or liposculpture) is performed with a small, delicate instrument called a cannula, which permanently siphons away unwanted fat. This procedure is commonly performed in conjunction with a face-lift and is also used to reduce jowls or pudgy cheeks. Some doctors are against removing fat in the cheeks. Fat loss in this area tends to be aging in future years. Also, achieving symmetry in the cheeks can be difficult.

New methods of suctioning the deeper layers of fat, as well as the layer of fat directly beneath the skin, have proven to circumvent the problems of skin depressions or irregularities. When not combined with a face-lift, though, suctioning works best for people under thirty. This procedure can be done in the office. This is beneficial to someone who is afraid to have a face-lift or simply doesn't have time to devote to the recovery period.

For neck contouring, a small incision, which fades in time, is normally made under the chin. Pressure bandages are worn afterward for better results. Recovery time is fast, but it may take several months for swelling to completely subside to fully appreciate the end result.

Chemical peel

A chemical peel is a scalpel-free form of cosmetic surgery that accomplishes many things that a face-lift cannot. Peels are used for *resurfacing* the skin to smooth wrinkles, crow's-feet, blemishes, scars, sun damage, freckles, and other discolorations. Peels won't reduce large pores or improve broken capillaries. A medium to deep chemical peel, although not a substitute for face-lifting, is sometimes referred to as a "non-surgical face-lift." Studies have shown that skin's elasticity can be improved up to twenty years after a deep peel.

Of all procedures, the chemical peel can produce one of the most dramatic results in facial rejuvenation and is one of the fastest growing cosmetic procedures today. Unless it's skillfully administered, however, results can be unpredictable and disappointing, and can lead to serious complications, such as scarring (particularly around the mouth), permanent reddening, skin lightening or darkening, broken capillaries, and an increase in skin sensitivity.

The ideal candidate for a peel is a fair- and thin-skinned, light-eyed individual. Darker skin has a tendency to permanently lighten with deep peels, especially on blacks and Asians. Deep peels aren't usually performed on men because of the possibility of skin lightening, causing a line of demarcation between the face and neck (women could correct this with foundation). Also, people who have had ultraviolet light treatment for acne scarring risk some pigment change because the skin is usually thinner and less elastic if extensive radiation was used.

Chemical peels range in strength from deep peels (using such solutions as phenol) to medium and light peels (using various milder acids such as trichloroacetic acid [TCA], glycolic acid, salicylic acid, lactic acid, and resorcinol). Some doc-

---

"I knew I looked old, but I didn't know what could be done. I thought about a face-lift, but the surgeon suggested a phenol peel instead. It didn't hurt as much as I thought and the redness looked worse than it felt. I didn't see anybody for about ten days. After three weeks, I went to a wedding. Everyone said I looked better and wanted to know why."

Barbara (age 70), <u>before</u> deep chemical peel (her makeup).

Six weeks <u>after</u> procedure (my makeup).

tors now customize peels by mixing and matching the different solutions on specific areas of the face (designer peels). For moderate sun damage, many doctors feel that two or three light to medium peels achieve better and safer results than one phenol peel. Superior results are believed to be obtained with preparatory steps such as a preoperative course of Retin-A (see "Retin-A: Miracle in a Jar?", page 71) to provide a deeper penetration of the solution and a more even result.

THE CHEMICAL PEEL PROCEDURE

Full face peels cover the entire face, with the exception of the brows and lips. Partial peels, or "spot" peels, treat the areas around the eyes, the vertical lines above the upper lip, or other specific areas of the face.

Both procedures involve painting the face (or a particular area of the face) with an acid-based chemical that burns away the top layer of skin. After the solution is applied, burning may be experienced. The pain quickly disappears since the chemical acts as an anesthetic.

Pain, tenderness, and swelling are common after a deep peel but will subside within four days. Sometimes the face is taped to allow the solution to penetrate deeper. When crusting falls off a few days later, the new skin will be smoother, firmer, and healthier, but will appear very red (ointments are sometimes used to prevent crusting and lessen discomfort). The redness gradually fades to a lighter pink over the next few weeks, and will remain pink for several months. Light makeup can be applied in less than two weeks or when approved by your physician. After a peel, the face will be very sensitive, particularly to the Sun, which must be avoided for at least six months to a year thereafter. Wearing sunscreen is a necessity.

Without makeup, it's easy to examine Barbara's skin texture. Her skin elasticity and muscle tone were quite good before chemical peel (top). But, six weeks later, her skin has a new baby-smooth surface (bottom).

THE 'FRESHENING' PEEL

Light peels, said to be the equivalent of a year of Retin-A (see "Retin-A: Miracle in a Jar?", page 71), can improve milder pigmentation problems and fine, superficial lines on the face, neck, and chest. It can improve texture, but it won't eliminate deep wrinkles.

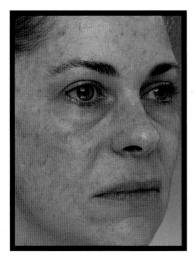

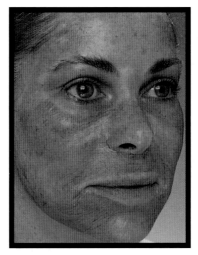

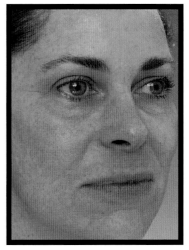

Paula (age 45), <u>before</u> light chemical peel (TCA): Her skin is virtually line-free, but because of photo-aging, it developed uneven pigmentation.

Two days <u>after</u> procedure: A light crust has formed.

One week <u>after</u> procedure: Crust has flaked off, revealing younger-looking, more even-toned skin.

One week <u>after</u> procedure (with makeup): Paula's skin takes on a glow she says she never had before. A sheer, liquid foundation is all that's necessary now for a flawless complexion.

Dermabrasion

Dermabrasion is particularly useful to even out pockmarked skin as well as to smooth out wrinkles in specific areas, such as the vertical lines around the mouth ("smoker's lines"). It may also diminish enlarged pores.

THE DERMABRASION PROCEDURE

Because of newer dermabrading techniques and equipment, dermabrasion is far superior now to the methods of the past. The procedure consists of "sanding" the area with a mechanical abrading instrument that flattens and smooths the surrounding skin. The results are similar in appearance to a deep peel. Reddened, fresh new skin will appear after a brief crusting period. The possibility of skin-lightening is somewhat less common than with a peel. Many doctors prefer this procedure for treating specific areas of the face (such as the upper lip), as well as for treating darker or olive-skinned individuals. Dermabrasion for deep acne scars is normally repeated in two or three stages, each about a year apart.

The recovery from dermabrasion is similar to that of a chemical peel.

CORRECTIVE MAKEUP AFTER CHEMICAL PEEL AND DERMABRASION

If redness is one-toned and uniform, a green color corrector used underneath a light-weight foundation will give the best results. (see photographs, page 27). Heavier coverage, such as camouflage cream, should be used instead, to help hide darker areas. To cover minor redness in small areas, a neutralizer is best. After deep peels, be sure to use clean applicators. Use cotton balls, at this time, instead of brushes to apply face powder and blusher. Be sure to check with your doctor before you start to wear makeup.

Facial fillers

Correcting defects caused by scarred, damaged, and aging skin can be accomplished with various facial fillers (called soft tissue augmentation).

Collagen injections

One of the most popular facial fillers is collagen. Injectable collagen (also referred to as collagen replacement therapy or collagen implants) can help rejuvenate the face by bringing back fullness to certain areas. Collagen (a purified protein derived from cowhide) is placed just beneath the skin's surface. Facial lines, creases, indentations, wrinkles, and scars can be lessened and sometimes eliminated by collagen's ability to take on the characteristic of surrounding tissue. Unfortunately, collagen isn't permanent and is eventually absorbed by the body.

Although collagen is approved by the FDA, about 3 percent of the population has an allergic reaction to collagen, and skin tests are required one month pior to treatment. Some doctors insist on double testing because reactions can occur even after tests show a negative result. There has been some speculation that injectable collagen may be linked to immune system disorders, but thus far there has been no evidence to demonstrate any causal relationship. Injectable human collagen is now being tested and showing favorable results.

Collagen treatments can take from two to four visits and last from four months to a year before touch-ups are needed.

Michael Maron __before__ collagen injections: "I've had smile lines since I was a teenager. Notice the crease from the outside corners of my nostrils to the outside corners of my mouth (nasolabial fold)."

One month __after__ procedure: "After two collagen treatments my smile lines are gone. . . at least temporarily."

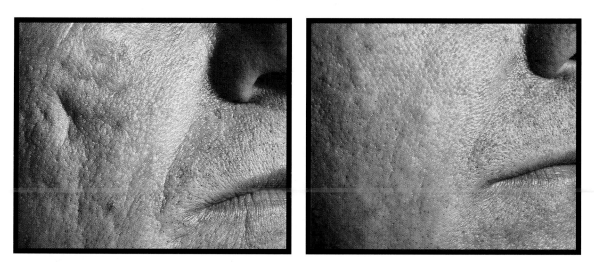

Collagen can fill scars or craters resulting from acne. For deeper "ice pick" scars, punch-grafting (skin from back of ear transplanted to face) and laser therapy can offer a permanent remedy (see "Scar Correction," page 109).

THE COLLAGEN INJECTION PROCEDURE

Collagen is offered in different degrees of thickness. The thinnest version is administered through a very small needle and can help fill in the fine lines (particularly crow's-feet) around the eyes. Thicker versions are used to fill deeper areas of the skin.

The procedure takes only a few moments to perform. Most people find the injections tolerable, although some people request topical anesthetics. The injected area may sting or throb slightly after the procedure, and redness usually disappears within twenty-four hours but can be corrected with neutralizer. Occasionally, small bruising occurs; this can be covered with camouflage cream.

FULLER LIPS WITH COLLAGEN

Lips tend to shrink with age and the borders gradually lose definition (see "How the Face Ages," page 75). Plumping the lips with collagen around the borders can help achieve a younger, "poutier" mouth (sometimes called "The Paris Lip"). This illusion of fuller, larger lips is obtained by building up the two vertical ridges between the upper lip and nose, as well as the border beneath the lower lip. Collagen for the lips lasts between two to four months.

Since the FDA doesn't approve injectable collagen for plumping the actual lips, fat injections can be used instead. Permanent fuller lips can be achieved by a surgery using an implant made from your own skin (called a dermal graft), or—newer on the horizon—a synthetic lip implant.

fat injections

Because fat injections are a newer method of facial filling, they're still referred to by many names: fat grafting, fat implants, fat transfer (or transplantation), autologous fat transplant, lipoplasty, or lipoinjection. Fat has the advantage over collagen of being nonallergenic because fat is a natural component of the body. It can be used to rejuvenate or contour the face. Fat is

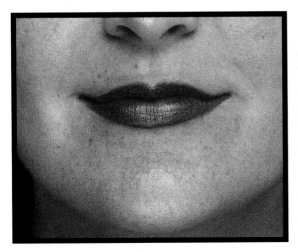

Before collagen injections.

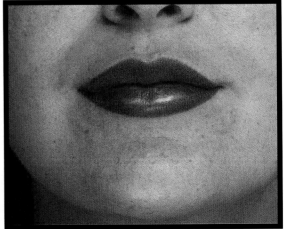

One month after procedure: Lips appear fuller, and vertical lines above upper lip are filled in with collagen to prevent lipstick from bleeding.

extracted from your own body (normally the abdomen, thighs, or buttocks) and injected into an area of the face. A local anesthetic is usually administered to numb the site of injection. The most common sites are depressions, laugh lines between the nose and mouth (the nasolabial fold), frown lines between the eyebrows, and forehead furrows. Swelling is more evident after treatment than with collagen injections. As with collagen injections, the results are temporary. Some doctors believe that approximately 20 percent of the fat is pepmanently retained after each treatment and advise multiple treatments in a given area for this reason. Fat injections administered during a face-lift are gaining in popularity. Redness and bruising are more common with collagen injections and can be covered with neutralizer or camouflage cream.

Silicone injections

Although nonallergenic and offering permanent results, liquid silicone (not to be confused with solid silicone implants) is still highly controversial. Doctors in favor of injectable silicone state that complications have arisen because of faulty technique and use of contaminated product. They believe silicone is an effective therapeutic approach to facial lines, wrinkles, and skin depressions as long as pure, medical-grade silicone is injected by the "micro-droplet" technique (minute amounts over a period of time).

Many doctors don't recommend injectable silicone because liquid silicone hasn't been approved for sale at this time by the FDA, and its use is illegal. Others who oppose its use say that silicone may be linked to autoimmune disease, that it may cause irreversible damage if it should migrate into surrounding tissues, lymph nodes, and other organs, and that problems can occur even years after treatment.

Fibrel

Fibrel is an injectable material made of natural gelatin derived from pigskin that's reconstituted with one's own blood plasma. An alternative for those allergic to collagen, Fibrel is known to actually activate the body's own collagen production to correct skin depressions (particularly scars). Absorption in the body is similar to that of injectable collagen. Repeated injections, however, show longer-term improvement than does collagen. Swelling and bruising usually subside in one to two days. Neutralizer and camouflage cream can help correct discoloration.

Cutting-edge wrinkle fixers and fill-ins

New facial fillers still awaiting FDA approval are showing promising results.

Gore-Tex, a synthetic material that won't deteriorate over time, is inserted with a needle, causing the body to form scar tissue around the threads of Gore-Tex. This can plump up the skin as much as 60 percent. Similarly, another permanent skin-plumper, called Bioplastique, an injectable microimplant containing tiny particles of silicone rubber (not liquid silicone), causes one's own collagen to surround the particles and be permanently fixed in place. Bioplastique is currently available in Europe. Presently, both materials show no risk of allergy.

A new alternative method of treating wrinkles incorporates the use of Botex, a drug used to treat muscle spasms that is a purified biological protein. When Botex is injected into wrinkles caused by the pull of facial muscles (such as frown lines or crow's-feet), the drug relaxes the muscles and reduces or completely eliminates the wrinkles. This is an almost painless procedure. The desired effect becomes visible in three to four days and lasts up to six months.

Other face-saving procedures

Many relatively simple office procedures (usually performed by a dermatologist) are available to improve the appearance of the skin. Some of the most common are *electrodesiccation*, *cryosurgery*, *laser therapy*, and *scar correction*.

ELECTRODESICCATION

Electrodesiccation (cauterization) consists of "zapping" the skin with a small electric needle. This procedure helps destroy red, broken capillaries; corrects various pigmentation problems; and eliminates raised areas of the skin (similar to localized dermabrasion). Other than a slight stinging sensation, little discomfort is felt because the needle is used for a split second. Tiny scabs form that fall off after a few days, leaving fresh, new skin. Minuscule red marks can remain for a couple of weeks; they can be covered with neutralizer.

CRYOSURGERY

Large freckles (liver spots), discolorations, and precancerous pigmentations resulting from sun damage can be improved with cryosurgery. Treatment consists of freezing the area with a small amount of liquid nitrogen. After treatment, the area dries up and flakes off in about a week, revealing new skin that's slightly reddened for a few weeks. Neutralizers can hide the redness.

LASER THERAPY

Lasers, which utilize amplified light of varied colors to treat the skin, have proven to be medical miracles over the past decade. Lasers, such as the carbon dioxide laser (CO_2) are now being used by some doctors to treat wrinkles, scars (see "Scar Correction," page 109), precancerous conditions, and skin cancer. After treatment, the area will be slightly red for a few hours and can be hidden by neutralizer. Discomfort is minimal.

The pulsed tunable dye laser (also known as the Candela laser), can successfully fade and sometimes remove birthmarks, such as port wine stains. It heats quickly, permitting localized treatment without damaging the surrounding skin (great success has been achieved with this type of laser in treating children with birthmarks). This type of laser effectively treats broken capillaries, pigmentary sports, acne rosacea, and strawberry patches (called hemangiomas) as well. The treated areas feel like a sunburn for only a few hours, then begin to turn purple for about two weeks. Camouflage cream can be used as a cover-up throughout this time.

The Q-switched ruby laser, the VAG laser, and the Alexandrite laser are revolutionary types of lasers used to remove previously indelible colors of tattoos (particularly blue, black, and brown). The ruby laser has shown equally impressive results with dark lesions and pigmentations, such as age spots, freckles, "café-au-lait" spots, and melasma (dark patches commonly occurring during pregnancy). Treatment with these lasers are tolerable with minimal discoloration. A sunburn-like effect will last for a few hours and is easily masked by neutralizers. At present, the Q-switched ruby laser and the Alexandrite aren't widely available.

Laser therapy, depending on the condition, consists of several five- to fifteen-minute sessions. Broken capillaries usually require two to four treatments, and more are needed for port wine stains. Slight stinging is experienced with each treatment.

Remarkable advances in laser therapy continue, but precaution is necessary since lasers can over-treat, creating skin discoloration, inflammation, and scarring.

COSMETIC SURGERY—A BEAUTY REVOLUTION

SCAR CORRECTION

By the time most people reach forty, they have a scar somewhere. Dermabrasion is best for depressed scars caused by acne (see "Dermabrasion," page 104). Results can be impressive, but correction is never perfect. Dermaplaning consists of shaving off the raised area of the scar with a razor to help flatten it. Grafting (implanting skin taken from another area) helps replace scarred, damaged, or depressed scars such as "ice pick" scars. Scar revision actually "redesigns" a scar, usually by creating a zigzag incision (called Z-plasty) to form a thinner scar. Cortisone injections can help smooth or shrink a scar but won't affect its color. Laser therapy, in the hands of a skilled doctor, can improve surgical, accidental, or acne scars. Acne scars are treated by directing the pinpointed laser beam around the edge of the scar's crater. Although a few treatments are usually needed, healing time is relatively quick. Deeper "ice pick" scars usually don't respond well. Facial fillers, such as collagen, are excellent for raising depressed areas, but are not permanent (see "Collagen Injections," page 104). Tattooing with flesh-colored dyes can help adjust the color of a scar (see "Permanent Makeup," page 58).

redefining facial features

Redefining the nose, chin, and cheeks (the three landmarks of the face) with cosmetic surgery can improve symmetry and affect one's overall appearance. The balance and harmony of these

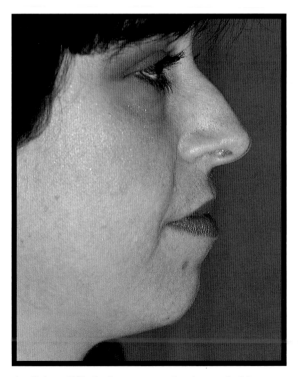

April (age 38), <u>before</u> nose reshaping and chin augmentation: A receding chin can make a nose appear even larger.

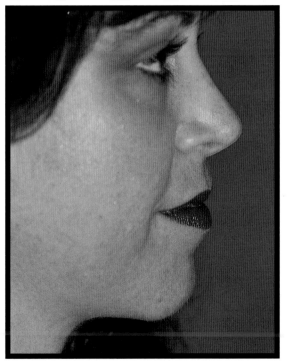

Four months <u>after</u> surgery: Features are more delicate, and in fact make April appear younger as well as prettier. Liposuction below chin, done in combination with a chin implant, produces a more sculpted jawline.

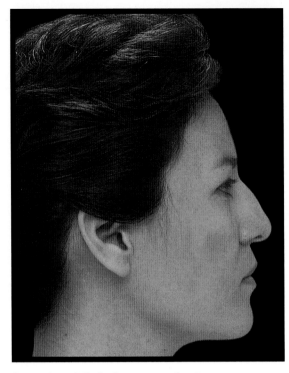

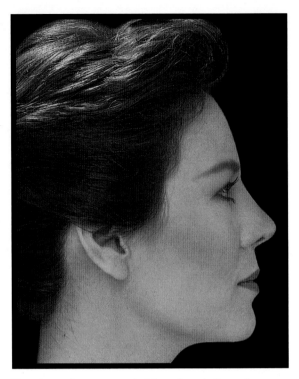

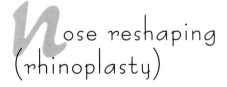

Laura (age 25), <u>before</u> nose reshaping.

Ten days <u>after</u> surgery (with makeup): Laura's new, more feminine nose is reshaped, but not any smaller.

Bridge is straightened and nasal angle raised (tip will drop slightly when swelling subsides). An implant (grafting) is placed at upper bridge of nose (where it joins forehead) and another implant is under base of nose (where nose joins upper lip)—to create a 90-degree angle. An implant to extend tip of nose is also used to improve facial proportion (otherwise a chopped-off or typical operated-on looking nose would result). This exemplifies skilled surgery.

dominant skeletal elements are responsible for our perception of facial beauty (see "Facial Harmony," page 16).

*n*ose reshaping (rhinoplasty)

Because the nose is situated in the middle of the face, it probably influences facial harmony more than any other feature. This is one of the reasons the cookie-cutter "nose job" of the late sixties and early seventies appeared so obviously "done," with its too small size, scooped bridge, pinched, upturned pointy tip, and flared nostrils.

These "BNJs" (bad nose jobs) were generally performed by qualified surgeons, who tended to practice the same methods on every face. With advanced techniques in nasal surgery that include newer grafting materials (implants), more precise control, and sophisticated approaches toward individual facial design, nose reshaping can now achieve very natural-looking results. Today, revisional surgeries are becoming more and more popular to improve and modernize these outdated noses. Still, approximately 5 percent of those who have had recent nasal surgery become repeat customers.

Because the nose drops as one ages, it can appear larger with time (see "How the Face Ages," page 75). Nasal surgery can raise the tip, which also can help achieve a younger appearance. And because of scar tissue within the nose, nasal surgery is said to permanently keep the nose from dropping.

Today, both men and women prefer a straight, "classic" nose with some nasal prominence, without an overly upturned tip (see "Nose Placement," page 18, and "The Well-Balanced Profile," page 19). The trend now is improvement, while preserving one's individuality and ethnicity, rather than radical change. No longer is a little nose the criterion for an aesthetically pleasing nose. Men, in particular, want strong, assertive-looking noses. In fact, I know of a male model who had the bridge of his nose surgically built up because he thought his nose was too "perfect." He claimed too many people thought his natural nose was a "nose job," which may have jeopardized his work.

Generally, many people assume the primary purpose of nose reshaping is to make a large nose smaller. In reality, most noses that appear large may not be large at all. Redesigning its shape can create the illusion of a smaller nose without necessarily reducing its size. Now surgeons try to reshape rather than remove. Traditionally, tissue was removed from the nose. Modern nose reshaping adds cartilage (typically from the ear), bone, or synthetic material to enlarge areas of the nose. Chin augmentation is usually done in tandem with nose reshaping because the chin plays such an integral part in how the nose is perceived (see "Chin Augmentation," page 115).

The nasal tip, ignored by many surgeons in the past, is a major influence on the aesthetic appearance of the nose. In fact, when the bridge of a hooked nose is reduced (called tip revision),

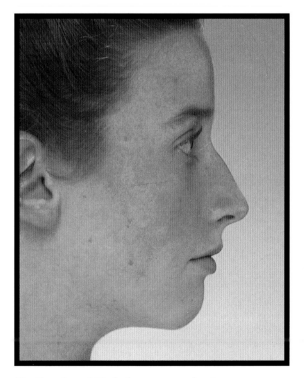

Heather (age 16), <u>before</u> nose reshaping: Undergoing nasal surgery at a young age can improve self-image and self-confidence.

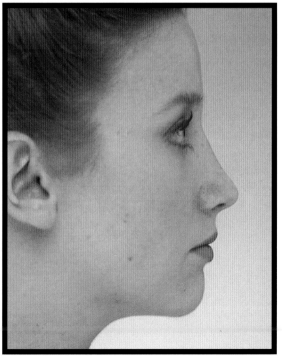

Eight days <u>after</u> surgery: Nasal hump is reduced as is angle where nose joins upper lip. Profile appears less convex. Subtle adjustments like these can create an illusion of a more prominent chin (her chin was never altered). Pretty Heather still looks like herself, only better.

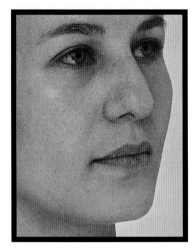

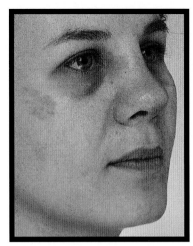

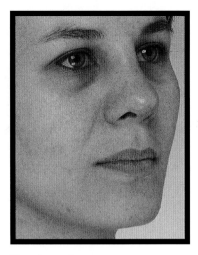

*Laura, **before** nose reshaping.*

Five days *after* surgery: Splint was just removed. Because Laura has thick skin, she's typical of someone who experiences more swelling after nose reshaping. Facial discoloration and black-and-blue marks around eyes are common.

Ten days *after* surgery: Discoloration is almost gone. Nose will remain swollen for a few weeks.

the tip must often be built up to increase tip projection (see photographs, page 110). Oftentimes, improvement of the nasal tip is all that's necessary for nose reshaping.

Teens particularly benefit from nose reshaping, but the surgery should only be performed when the nose is near full development (about fifteen years old for girls, sixteen for boys). It's important that the teen request the surgery rather than the parent or doctor (see photographs, page 111).

THE NOSE RESHAPING PROCEDURE

Normally, incisions are made inside the nose, where the surgeon works on reshaping and modifying the cartilage and bones. Depending on the individual, nose refinements can be performed without having to break the nose; but breaking the bones is frequently necessary to bring all parts of the nose into balance (particularly when the bridge of the nose is wide).

After surgery, most people experience some discomfort but little pain. An internal dressing (packing) is sometimes inserted in the nostrils to support the nose. A small splint (or cast) is usually worn for five to seven days. After both are removed, the nose may appear overly turned up, but it will gradually drop. Swelling and bruising depend on how aggressive the surgical techniques were and on one's own physiology (see top photographs, page 34). When a wide nose is surgically narrowed it can temporarily appear to be even wider following surgery. Most swelling subsides within three or four days after the splint or bandage is removed. Generally, thicker-skinned individuals remain swollen longer. The majority of swelling is gone in about four months, but it can take a full year (and as long as two years for people with thick skin) for the nose to completely take form. Because incisions are usually internal, there's no visible scarring.

Recovery is relatively quick. Most people are back to work within one to two weeks. Makeup can be worn as soon as bandages are removed. Tinted glasses can also help hide discoloration, bruising, and puffy eyes. If you wear glasses, avoid resting them on the bridge of your nose for about eight weeks. Instead, suspend the glasses with athletic tape. Wrap one end of a piece of tape around the bridge of the glasses and tape other end to your forehead.

CORRECTIVE MAKEUP AFTER NOSE RESHAPING

Highlighter and contour shadow can temporarily improve the appearance of swelling and give the illusion of how the nose might look when most of the swelling subsides. Camouflage cream can hide any discoloration.

*TOP LEFT: **Before** makeup: Ten days after nose reshaping, nose and face are swollen from procedure. Some discoloration remains around eyes.*

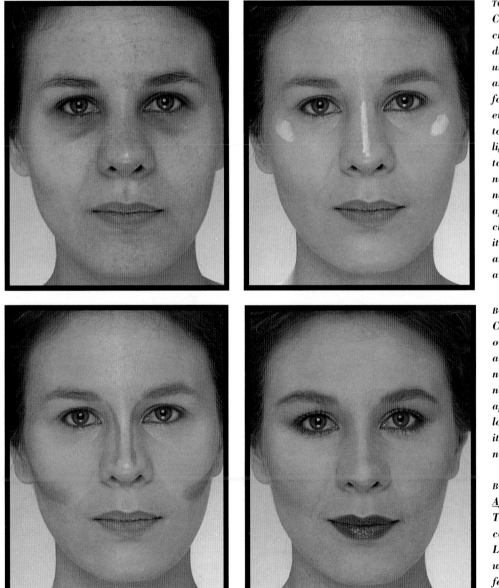

TOP RIGHT: Camouflage cream hides discoloration under eyes, and normal foundation evens out skin tone. High-lighter applied to bridge of nose helps to narrow; when applied to cheekbones, it brings angularity to a puffy face.

BOTTOM LEFT: Contour shad-ow applied along sides of nose helps to narrow; when applied to hol-low of cheeks, it reduces full-ness.

BOTTOM RIGHT: After makeup: This is an indi-cation of how Laura's nose will look in a few months.

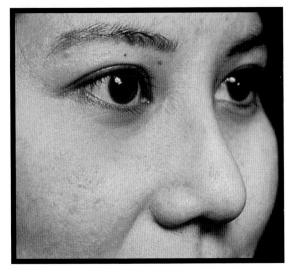

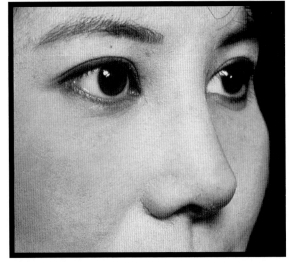

Twenty-eight-year-old Asian-American woman __before__ nose reshaping. A wide bridge and flat tip are common with Asian noses.

One year __after__ surgery: Noses can be adjusted with surgery utilizing implants. It's very important that adjustments be subtle and retain inherent ethnic characteristics.

"My nose always bothered me. I was called `beak´ in school. I only wish I hadn´t waited until I was twenty-three to have it done."

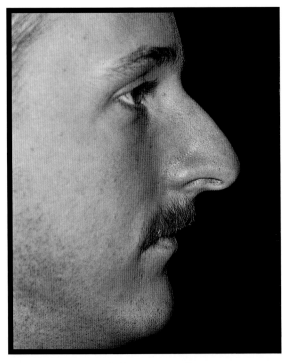

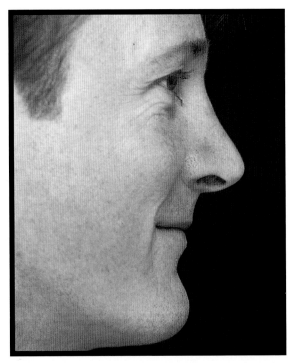

Richard (age 31), __before__ nose reshaping.

Eight years __after__ surgery: Richard's new nose and chin implant make him look younger now than he did eight years ago when his surgery was performed. He wore a mustache to draw less attention to his convex profile.

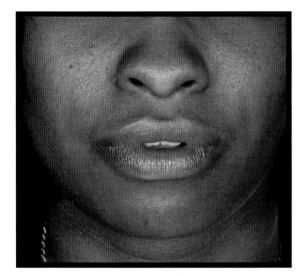

Twenty-three-year-old African-American woman before nose reshaping.

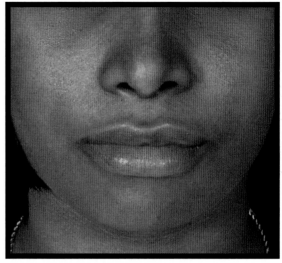

One year after surgery: Bridge of nose has more definition. This should never be overdone. A wider nose is more appropriate on blacks. Ethnic heritage should still be maintained while enhancing beauty.

facial implants

The architecture of the face can be improved by recontouring the actual shape of the face with implants. As one ages, the bones in the face shrink a bit (see "How the Face Ages," page 75). Facial implants can solve this underlying problem that a face-lift can't.

Most facial implants are made of a solid, flexible silicone rubber (called silastic) that's different than the silicone gel used in breast implants. So far, research has shown no clear evidence of any danger from solid silicone.

Chin augmentation (mentoplasty)

The lower third of the face has always been a determining factor in facial aesthetics. A smooth, continuous jawline plays an important role in facial beauty (see left photograph, page 16).

Rarely do we see ourselves in profile, so if we have a facial imbalance, most of us would be unaware that it could be attributed to the size or shape of our chin (see "The Well-Balanced Profile," page 19). Small or receding chins can undermine the entire face, causing the nose to look large (see bottom left photograph, page 114), the mouth to have an overbite, or the jawline to appear to have a double chin. Chin implants can remedy this as well as offer additional facial improvements.

For narrow faces or weak jawlines, customized jaw implants are now available that can actually widen the face. Shifting of the implant is one possible risk, due to movement in this part of the face. Over-augmentation of the chin area (particularly if the width of the upper portion of the face is narrow) can defeat its purpose and can sometimes create a "horsey" appearance. As with all implants placed over bony areas, there's a possibility of bone shrinkage (called bone absorption). Doctors don't perceive this to be a serious consideration, having observed the results of facial implants for more than sixty years.

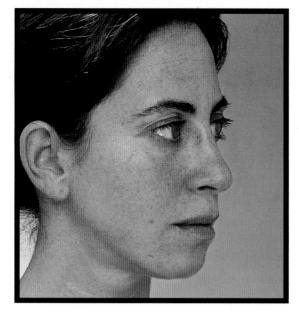

Bonnie (age 30), <u>before</u> chin augmentation.

Two months <u>after</u> surgery (with makeup): Bonnie decided to combine chin augmentation with eyelid surgery (upper lids only).

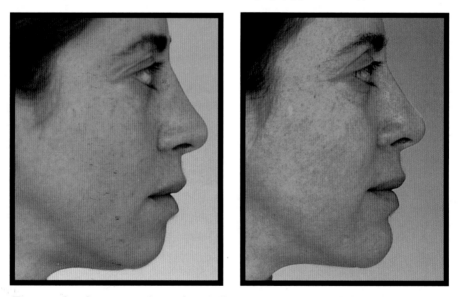

Two months <u>after</u> surgery (no makeup): Features appear more balanced (particularly her nose) because of chin augmentation.

In some cases, with conventional chin implants, improvement is apparent from the profile, but the chin can appear to jut forward from the front, creating an unnatural, pointy look. A new development in chin augmentation, the anatomic extended chin implant, or chin-jowl implant, is a customized implant that conforms to the shape of the chin and slightly wraps onto the jawline to create a squarer, stronger-looking jaw. A moldable material called hydroxyapatite, commonly used by maxillofacial and oral surgeons, is sometimes used for this purpose. Custom chin implants, combined with skillful stitching technique, can create cleft chins.

THE CHIN AUGMENTATION PROCEDURE

The implant is inserted in a pocket between the bone and soft tissues through a short incision made underneath the chin (or sometimes inside the mouth) that soon becomes barely detectable. Swelling is common for about two weeks and is the reason some people think their implant is bigger than it actually is. Swelling (and numbness) may take a few months to totally disappear. Infections can occur with implants, and sometimes the implant has to be removed or replaced.

Symmetry of the lower face can also be improved with orthognathic surgery (oral surgery that straightens recessive or protruding bites), which is typically performed by an oral or maxillofacial surgeon. Other asymmetries of the face, such as long-face syndrome, can also be corrected by changing the underlying bone structures. This too, is usually done by an oral or maxillofacial surgeon, as well as a craniofacial surgeon.

Cheek augmentation (malarplasty)

Although high cheekbones have always been a determining factor in facial attractiveness, the cheekbones can also help make a face appear younger by raising the upper part of the face. With today's improvements in implant design, and use of computers, the architecture of the entire face can be enhanced more naturally. Cheek implants (called malar implants) now conform to the size and shape of the natural cheekbone, whereas once they were made too large to achieve normal projection. Anatomic zonal concepts dictate where augmentation can benefit the face; this once was a problem for overzealous surgeons who obtained unnatural angularity and over-projection from improper positioning of implants. Cheek augmentation can also improve the result of flattened cheeks that sometimes occurs when the skin is repositioned by a face-lift.

Dianne (age 51), <u>before</u> mid-face implants: Although Dianne has pretty features, overly hollow cheeks make her face appear gaunt.

Two months <u>after</u> surgery: Even though eyelid surgery helped rejuvenate Dianne's face, mid-face implants plump out cheeks for a more youthful look.

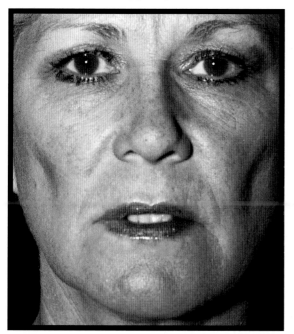

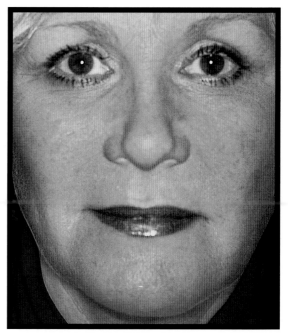

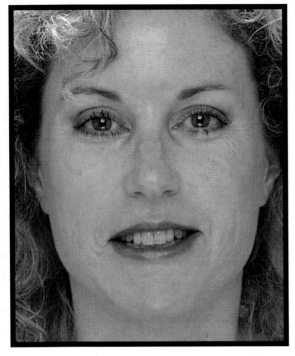

Joanne (age 43), <u>before</u> cheek augmentation (her makeup).

Three months <u>after</u> surgery (my makeup): Joanne's subtle result brings more angularity to her face.

"As I approached forty, my face began to drop. I always attributed high cheekbones to the beauty of the actresses whose faces I admired. I decided to get the implants at the same time I had the tip of my nose narrowed. At first, when I smiled, it felt like something artificial was there. Now I can't feel it at all."

Since fuller cheeks are indicative of youth, cheekbone augmentation can sometimes compound the problem of a very thin face with hollow cheeks. Cheekbone augmentation can sometimes make the face appear too skeletal and actually age the face. Mid-face (middle third of the face) implants, called submalar implants, solve the problem of a gaunt or sunken cheek, typical of people in their fifties. Because of facial bone shrinkage, loss of dental support, muscle shrinkage, collagen loss, and surrounding fatty tissue being pulled down by gravity, the middle part of the face is one of the first to show serious signs of aging (see "How the Face Ages," page 75). Conventional face-lifts performed on someone with very hollow cheeks can sometimes create a masklike appearance unless the procedure is combined with mid-face augmentation or fat transplants (see "Fat Injections," page 106). In fact more and more surgeons speculate that augmentation of the mid-face will soon become fundamental to face-lifts.

Shells, which are implants that combine upper and mid-face implants in one piece, can give the face added cheekbone prominence, and can plump up the cheek area as well. The shells

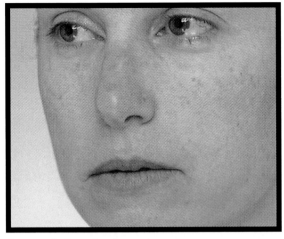

Joanne, before cheek augmentation.

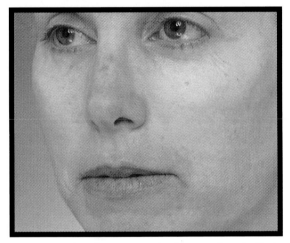

Three months after surgery (without makeup): Notice higher prominence of cheekbone. Cheekbone augmentation should always be subtle.

Three months after surgery (with makeup): Joanne's new cheekbones are further enhanced with makeup.

seem to offer the most successful result because of their ability to integrate the mid-face with the upper face. Caution must be taken for men considering cheek augmentation. Over-projection of either cheekbone or mid-face implants can feminize face.

THE CHEEK AUGMENTATION PROCEDURE

Cheek augmentation is generally performed through an incision made inside the mouth or through an incision placed just below the lower lashes, or through a face-lift incision. Implants can also be inserted at the time of a forehead-lift. Matching the two sides for symmetry is one of the trickiest aspects of the operation. The submalar implant poses the possible risk of shifting because its placement is a difficult area to position. There's minimal postoperative pain, with numbness and swelling lasting about five days, although it may take many months for swelling to disappear completely. Bruising and discoloration can easily be covered with camouflage cream.

BREAKTHROUGH IMPLANTS

Customized implants can also bring prominence to a slanted (recessed) forehead. There's even a small, flat, shield-shaped implant to smooth out frown lines (it is inserted through a tiny incision in the brow) and an implant to fill in the recessed area under the eye.

Combined with facial rejuvenation procedures, implants can help reestablish balance and harmony to the face.

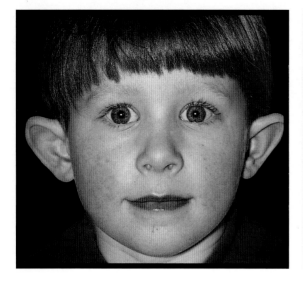

Steven (age 6), <u>before</u> ear correction.

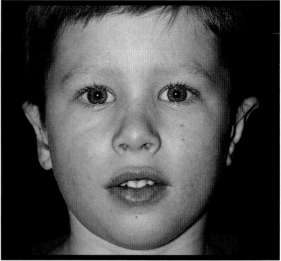

One year <u>after</u> surgery: Steven's protruding ears are corrected for life, eliminating potential psychological trauma.

ear correction (otoplasty)

Protruding ears are far more common than large ears. Although the problem is easily corrected at any age, ear surgery is ideally recommended for children as they near total ear development (after age four). As with all cosmetic procedures, however, ear surgery should never be performed on children until *they* express a desire to fix the problem.

Earlobe reductions can also help change the proportion of the ear itself (see "The Face-Lift Procedure," page 95).

EAR CORRECTION PROCEDURE

Pinning the ears back consists of removing some of the cartilage behind the ears and suturing it together. Incisions are concealed in a natural skin crease. Symmetry between both ears is difficult to achieve, but most people are incapable of noticing a slight difference. Throbbing is common after surgery for a couple of days and the ears may be swollen and red, but this gradually fades during the next few months. The ears are bandaged for several days and stitches are normally removed about a week later. Adults can go back to work about five days later, and children may need to wait a week before going back to school. Strenuous activity and sports can be resumed after a few weeks. Ear correction produces dramatic and immediate results that last a lifetime.

Resources

You can obtain additional information on some of the topics mentioned in this book by contacting the following organizations.

American Academy of Dermatology
P.O. Box 681069
Schaumburg, IL 60168-1069
(708) 330-0230

American Burn Association
New York Hospital Burn Center
525 East 68 Street, Room L706
New York, NY 10021
(800) 548-BURN

The Cleft Palate Foundation
1218 Grandview Avenue
Pittsburgh, PA 15211
(800) 24-CLEFT

Interplast, Inc.
2458 Embarcadero Way
Palo Alto, CA 94303
(415) 424-0123

National Alopecia Areata Foundation
P.O. Box 150760
San Rafael, CA 94915-0760
(415) 456-4644

National Vascular Malformation
    Foundation, Inc.
8320 Nightingale Street
Dearborn Heights, MI 48127
(313) 274-1243

National Vitiligo Foundation, Inc.
P.O. Box 6337
Tyler, TX 75711
(903) 534-2925

Operation Smile International
717 Boush Street
Norfolk, VA 23510
(804) 625-0375

The Phoenix Society for Burn
    Survivors, Inc.
11 Rust Hill Road
Levittown, PA 19056
(800) 888-BURN

Skin Cancer Foundation
245 Fifth Avenue, Suite 2402
New York, NY 10016
(212) 725-5176

COSMETIC SURGERY

American Academy of Cosmetic
    Surgery (AACS)
401 North Michigan Avenue
Chicago, IL 60611
(800) 221-9808

American Academy of Facial
    Plastic and Reconstructive
    Surgery (AAFPRS)
1110 Vermont Avenue NW,
    Suite 220
Washington, D.C. 20005
(800) 332-FACE

American Board of Medical
    Specialties (ABMS)
1 Rotary Center, Suite 805
Evanston, IL 60201
(800) 776-CERT

American Society for Aesthetic
    Plastic Surgery (ASAPS)
444 East Algonquin Road, Suite 110
Arlington Heights, IL 60005
(800) 635-0635

American Society of Plastic and
    Reconstructive Surgeons
    (ASPRS)
444 East Algonquin Road,
    Suite 200
Arlington Heights, IL 60005
(800) 635-0635

American Society for
    Dermatological Surgery (ASDS)
930 North Meacham Road
Schaumburg, IL 60173
(800) 441-2737

SUPPORT NETWORKS AND OTHER HELPFUL PROGRAMS

AboutFace USA
P.O. Box 737
Warrington, PA 18976
(800) 225-FACE

Let's Face It
P.O. Box 711
Concord, MA 01742
(508) 371-3186

Look Good . . . Feel Better
CTFA Foundation
1107 17 Street, Suite 300
Washington, D.C. 20036
(800) 395-LOOK

For private consultations with Michael Maron:

Michael Maron
P.O. Box 5061
Beverly Hills, CA 90209-0061
(213) 4-MAKEUP

Acknowledgments

Without the following people there would be no *Makeover Miracles*.

I'd like to thank the subjects whose naked faces grace these pages. And to the following well-known faces who agreed to appear in the book, I'm sincerely appreciative: Carmen, Gloria DeHaven, Phyllis Diller, Courtney Gibbs Eplin, Cristina Ferrare, Cassandra Peterson, Juliet Prowse, and Sally Struthers.

This book would probably not be in your hands if it weren't for my dear friend Linda Zimmerman, who insisted I write it, taught me how to use WordPerfect, and went on to make my words more perfect.

My thanks go to my agent extraordinaire, Barbara Lowenstein, who wanted this book even before she met me.

A big thank you to my editor Jane Meara for her astute criticism, to Ken Sansome, my art director, for his quality work, and to Lauren Dong for a beautiful book design. Thanks to Laurie Stark, Nancy Maynes, Kim Hertlein, Liddy Kelly, and Janet McDonald, at Crown, for their editorial support and dedicated work.

I'm grateful to Cristina Carlino for her knowledge, friendship, and belief in this book (and belief in me).

Special thanks to Elizabeth Sadati and Nancy Kobus and the American Society for Aesthetic Plastic Surgery, and Pamela Rasmussen and the American Society of Plastic and Reconstructive Surgeons, Jeff Knezovch, Julie Panos, Fred Newton, Cathey McMann-Newell and Kimberly Davey and the American Academy of Cosmetic Surgery, Judith Marden and the American Academy of Facial Plastic and Recon-structive Surgery, and Nadine Tosk, and the American Society of Dermatological Surgery.

I'm especially indebted to the following distinguished physicians, who shared their knowledge and patients: Patrick Abergel, M.D.; Robert Amonic, M.D.; Morton Bard, M.D.; Bruce Bauer, M.D; Mark Berman, M.D.; William Binder, M.D.; Mel Bircoll, M.D.; Fredric Brandt, M.D.; George Brennen, M.D.; Karen Burke, M.D.; Michael Churukian, M.D.; Sydney Coleman, M.D.; Bruce Connell, M.D.; Eugene Courtiss, M.D.; Robert Cucin, M.D.; William Dorfman, D.D.S.; David Duffy, M.D.; Ellison Edwards, M.D.; Richard Ellenbogen, M.D.; Robert Erseck, M.D.; Leslie Farkas, M.D.; Robert Flowers, M.D.; Jack Friedland, M.D.; Peter Goldman, M.D.; Ronald Goldstein, D.D.S.; Frederick Grazer, M.D.; Pearl Grimes, M.D.; Jack Gunter, M.D.; Robert Hutcherson, M.D.; John Joseph, M.D.; Raj Kanodia, M.D.; Arnold Klein, M.D.; Albert Kligman, M.D.; Lawrence Koplin, M.D.; Robert Kotler, M.D.; Norman Leaf, M.D.; Lawrence Lefkoff, M.D.; Evan Libaw, M.D.; Ronald Linder, M.D.; Nicholas Lowe, M.D.; Jeffrey Marmelzat, M.D.; Earl Matory, Jr., M.D.; Ronald Matsunaga, M.D.; Peter McKinney, M.D.; Paul McKissock, M.D.; Timothy Miller, M.D.; Harry Mittelman, M.D.; Richard Mladick, M.D.; David Morrow, M.D.; Howard Murad, M.D.; Robert Nemeroff, M.D.; Hunt Neurohr, M.D.; Julius Newman, M.D.; Michael Niccole, M.D.; Brian Novack, M.D.; Norman Orentreich, M.D.; Russel Pardoe, M.D.; Jon Perlman, M.D.; Jon Peterson, M.D.; Michael Pertschuk, M.D.; Nelson Powell, M.D.; Lawrence Reed, M.D.; Lawrence Rivkin, M.D.; Elliott Rose, M.D.; Sheldon Rosenthal, M.D.; Leo Rozner, M.D.; Michael Sachs, M.D.; Norman Shapiro, M.D.;

Adrianna Scheibner, M.D.; Lawrence Seifert, M.D.; Dennis Thompson, M.D.; Edward Terino, M.D.; Luiz Toledo, M.D.; Linton Whitaker, M.D.; David White, M.D.; James Williams, M.D.; John Williams, M.D.; and John Yarborough, Jr., M.D.

My heartfelt thanks go to the late Dr. George Musser, whose dedication and love for medicine will always be remembered by his colleagues, patients, and friends.

Thanks go to the following special individuals who contributed their time and information: Kathleen Barron, Linda Brandolisio, Jerry Brennen, Alan Breslau, Karen Burns, Mary Burris, David Buss, Skip Carter, Daniel Clark, Michael Cunningham, Virginia Cunningham, Cristophe, Lenore Cuyler, Tina Dawn, Vincent DeMarco, Rebecca Edwardson, Stephen Franzoi, Robert Gats, Barbara Gautier, Mark Goss, Susan Graham, Bruce Grant, Lynda Hirsch, Patricia Jimenez, Jordan James, Rebecca James, Peggy Knight, Kevin Kolarik, Norman Kurz, Frank Liberman, Allen Locklin, Marco, Sheila May, Charles Mizelle, Gail Peterson, Barbara Kammerer Quayle, Gabriel Ramirez, Jared Scheidman, Marjorie Hansen Shaevitz, Susan Terino, Frank Tiszai, Jim Van Der Keyl, Ingrid Vanderstok, Betsy Wilson, Bonnie Zabel, Alayne Zatulove, and Robin Zucker.

To my loving friends for their abiding encouragement, inspiration, and support, who are the true miracles in my life: Kinne Amonie, Peter Anthony, Kitty Bartholemew, Robert Biale, Susan Brodsky, Karen Cadle, Rhonda Carr, Michael Chapman, Richard Corbett, Fay DeWitt, Milly Ericson, Sandra Field, Laura Figueroa, Jim Foster, Gregory Gershuni, Judy Gray, Betty Grazer, Ole Henriksen, Laurie Huggins, Merryl Jaye, Peter Johnson, Loni Kallay, Arlen Kane, Tim Kennedy, John Kirby, Barbara Lauren, John Livesay, Bradley Look, Richard Margolis, Bruce Masters, Ralph Mehecidith, Diane McNabb, Mark McNabb, Peggy Mellody, Naimie Ojeil, Cathy Palmer, Craig Peralta, Frank Redzich, Laurence Roberts, Paul Rodriguez, Eric Root, Joan Ryan, Esther Spencer, Shirley Sullivan, Doug Swander, Wendi Tolkin, Kathy Tracy, Hillary Turk, Judy Varon, Gayiel Von, Timothy Wayne, Lucien Wolff, and Terry Wormwood.

I'd like to thank David Funt and Roslyn Baws for many years of shared ideas and creativity. I'm grateful for their time, talent, and friendship.

I thank my parents, Della and Joseph, and my favorite doctor—my brother Dr. Howard Maron—and my sister-in-law Ginger for being there when I needed them the most.

Credits

Page 22, bottom photograph: David Goldner

Page 27; page 88; page 90, bottom photographs; page 97; pages 101–102; page 116; pages 118–119: Courtesy of Dr. John Williams, Los Angeles, Calif.

Page 34, top photographs: Courtesy of Dr. George Musser, Los Angeles, Calif.

Page 60, top photographs: Courtesy of Dr. Elliott Rose, New York, N.Y.

Page 63: Courtesy of Dr. Pearl Grimes, Los Angeles, Calif.

Page 66: Sir Norman Parkinson.

Page 74, top right and bottom photograph: Electronic Photo Manipulation—Daniel Clark.

Page 86: Courtesy of Dr. David Morrow, Rancho Mirage, Calif.

Page 90, top photograph: Stephen Harvey.

Page 91, middle photographs: Courtesy of Dr. Robert Amonic, Santa Monica, Calif. (Photographs: Dr. Robert Amonic)

Page 91, bottom photographs; page 92, top photographs; page 95: Courtesy of Dr. Richard Ellenbogen, Los Angeles, Calif. (Photographs: Dr. Richard Ellenbogen)

Page 92, bottom photographs; page 98; page 114, top photographs: Courtesy of Dr. Robert Flowers, Honolulu, Hawaii. (Photographs: Dr. Robert Flowers)

Page 93: Courtesy of Dr. James Williams, Los Angeles, Calif.

Page 94: Courtesy of Dr. Robert Amonic, Santa Monica, Calif.

Page 99: Courtesy of Dr. Edward Terino, Agoura, Calif.

Page 100: Courtesy of Dr. George Musser, Los Angeles, Calif. (Photographs: Dr. George Musser)

Page 103: Courtesy of Ole Henriksen, Los Angeles, Calif.

Page 105, top photographs: Courtesy of Dr. Peter Goldman, Los Angeles, Calif.

Page 105, bottom photographs: Courtesy of Collagen Corporation, Palo Alto, Calif. (Photographs: Collagen Corporation)

Page 106: Courtesy of Dr. Lawrence Lefkoff, Beverly Hills, Calif. (Photographs: Dr. Lawrence Lefkoff)

Page 109: Courtesy of Dr. Robert Nemeroff, Beverly Hills, Calif. (Photographs: Dr. Robert Nemeroff)

Page 111: Courtesy of Dr. Raj Kanodia, Los Angeles, Calif.

Page 114, bottom photographs: Courtesy of Dr. Raj Kanodia, Los Angeles, Calif. (Photographs: Dr. Raj Kanodia)

Page 115: Courtesy of Dr. Earl Matory, Jr., Worcester, Mass. (Photographs: Dr. Earl Matory, Jr.)

Page 117: Courtesy of Dr. William Binder, Los Angeles, Calif. (Photographs: Dr. William Binder)

Page 120: Courtesy of Dr. Bruce Bauer, Chicago, Ill. (Photographs: Dr. Bruce Bauer)

Index

Cheekbones, 15, *36*, 37, 117, 118
Cheeks
    augmentation *see* Malarplasty
    correcting, 57–58
    redefining, 109
Chemabrasion *see* Chemical peel
Chemical peel, 83, *86*, *101*,
    101–102, *103*
Cher, 17, 67
Chin
    augmentation *see* Mentoplasty
    makeup for different types, *38*
    in profile, 19, 20
    see also Double chin
Chin-jowl implant, 116
Choice, 10
Cleft lip/palate, *64*
Collagen
    and Fibrel, 107
    fuller lips with, 106
    growth of, 71
    injections, 83, 104, *105*, 106
Color correctors, 25, *26*, 27, *27*
Color makeup
    choosing colors, 42–43
    correcting eyes, *42*, 43–50, *45*,
        46–47, *48*
    definition of, 41
    three dimensions of color, 41–42
Complementary color, 41–42
Computer imaging, 84
Concave profile, 20
Concealer, 27–29, *28*, *70*
Contour shadow, 35, *36*, 37, *37*,
    38, 39, *61*, *70*, 113, *113*
Convex profile, 20
Coronal-lift *see* Coronoplasty
Coronoplasty, 82, 87, *92*, 97–98,
    98, *99*
Corrective makeup, 11, *22*, *40*
    for burns, *60–61*
    after chemical peel and derma-
        brasion, 104
    and cosmetic surgery, 9, 80, 85
    to counteract, 25–27
    to cover, 27–35
    to create, 35–39
    "don'ts," 69

after eyelid surgery, 89, *99*
after face-lift, *94*, 97
as illusion, 23–39
instant face-lift, 68–69
makeup artist's secrets, 24
for mature woman, 68–69, *69–71*
after nose reshaping, 113, *113*
taking ten years off with, 69,
    70–71
see also specific types of makeup
Cortisone, 109
Cosmetics *see* Color makeup;
    Corrective makeup; specific
    cosmetics
Cosmetic surgery
    consultation, 84–85
    and corrective makeup, 9, 80, 85
    decision to have, 85
    finding a surgeon, 81, 84
    procedures, 11, 82–83
    realistic expectations, 81
    rebuilding and resurfacing, 87,
        101
    temporary aftereffects, 85
    what to expect, 85
    see also specific procedures, e.g.,
        Rhinoplasty
Cream blusher, 58
Crease, of eye, 43, *45*
Cryosurgery, 108

Deep peels, 101, 102, 104
Define and accent principle, 35,
    58
DeHaven, Gloria, 69, *69*
Deneuve, Catherine, 67
Depilatories, 57
Dermabrasion, 83, 104, 109
Dermapigmentation *see* Permanent
    makeup
Dermaplaning, 109
Dietrich, Marlene, 17
Diller, Phyllis, 78, *79*, 80, *80*
Discoloration, 29–35, *30*, *31*, *32*,
    33, *34*, 85
Distinctiveness, 17
Double chin, 37, *37*
Dyer, Wayne, 10

Ear correction *see* Otoplasty
Electrodessication, 108
Electrolysis, 53, *56*, 57, 68
Evans, Linda, 67
Exfoliants, 39
Extrinsic aging, 77
Eyebrows, 46, 50–51, *51*, *56*, *63*
    balance, 51
    color, 52
    down-slanting, *51*
    drawing on, *61*
    grooming, 53
    height, 51–52
    hints, 53
    permanent makeup, 58, *59*
    realistic, *52*
    shape, 52, *71*
    thickness, 52
Eyelash curler, 49
Eyelashes, 49–50, 58, *59*, *63*, 68
Eyelid, 43, *45*
    surgery *see* Blepharoplasty
Eyeliner, 44, *59*
Eye pencil, 43, 44, *45*
Eyes, 15
    accenting, 43, *45*, 46, *71*
    bags under, *38*, 39, *70*, 89
    circles under, 27–29, *28*, *70*
    correcting with color makeup,
        42, 43–50, *45*, *46–47*, *48*
    creams for, 39
    defining, 43, *45*, 45–46, *70*
    lining, 43, 44–45, *45*, *70*
    "map," *43*
    placement of, 18
    types of, 46–48, *46–48*
    see also specific eye makeup,
        e.g., Mascara
Eye shadow, 42, *42*, 43–44, *45*,
    45–46, 47–48, *93*

Face analysis, 17–20
Face-lift *see* Rhytidectomy
Face shape, 17
Facial architecture, 17
Facial attractiveness, *16*, 17
Facial calibrator, 17